Blackstone's Guide to

CONTAMINATED LAND

Blackstone's Guide to

CONTAMINATED LAND

Trevor Hellawell

BLACKSTONE
PRESS LIMITED

First published in Great Britain 2000 by Blackstone Press Limited,
Aldine Place, London W12 8AA. Telephone (020) 8740 2277
www.blackstonepress.com

© Trevor Hellawell, 2000

ISBN: 1 84174 142 6

British Library Cataloguing in Publication Data
A CIP catalogue record for this book is available from the British Library.

Typeset by Montage Studios Limited, Horsmonden, Kent
Printed and bound in Great Britain by Antony Rowe Limited, Chippenham and
Reading

Contents

Preface

Trying to write any book which is intended to simplify such a complex piece of legislation as Part IIA of the Environmental Protection Act 1990 on contaminated land was never going to be easy.

Too much detail and you end up rewriting the primary materials — probably less well than the original drafters — too little and your contribution misses some vital piece of detail which underpins the whole thing.

I hope I have got the balance about right, and that my comments help to illuminate the debate on this important new attempt to improve and preserve our landmass for future generations.

My thanks go to all those professional colleagues with whom I have had the pleasure of discussing the legislation in the many years since it was first mooted, in particular Paul Winter, Nick Lightbody and our colleagues on the Law Society's Planning and Environmental Law Committee.

I am also grateful to the staff of Blackstone Press for their enthusiasm, encouragement and assistance.

The errors which remain, and the views expressed, are my own.

Trevor Hellawell
June 2000

Abbreviations

CL(E)R 2000	Contaminated Land (England) Regulations 2000
DETR	Department of the Environment, Transport and the Regions
EPA 1990	Environmental Protection Act 1990
Guidance	DETR Circular on Contaminated Land
IPC	integrated pollution control
para.	paragraph
PPC	pollution prevention and control
Pt	Part
reg.	regulation
s.	section
sch.	schedule
SPL	significant pollutant linkage

Chapter 1
Contaminated Land: General Introduction

BACKGROUND

The issue of contaminated land has bedevilled successive governments for years. The latest manifestation of the legislation intended to deal with it was first introduced in 1990, and the intervening years have been spent trying to refine the system and knock it into an acceptable — that is to say, workable — shape.

Even before that, though, many diverse suggestions were made in an attempt to deal with the UK's legacy of tainted ground. Being at the forefront of an industrial revolution and two world wars has left the UK with a significant stock of land which contains a variety of substances which one could class as polluting, poisonous or dangerous in some sense. The perennial question is what to do about it.

After many false starts, the UK Government announced in the 1993 White Paper, 'Paying for our Past', the essential policy parameters that would guide its future thinking on how to deal with contaminated land. These were:

- the prevention of further contamination at source
- the promotion of sustainable development
- the suitable for use approach (cleaning land up only to the standard required for its intended use, not any use (the 'polished earth' policy favoured by some other jurisdictions))
- the polluter pays principle (that the polluter of the land should pay to clean it up)
- the notions that
  - all clean-up steps should be cost-effective
  - only those sites which pose a real risk of danger should be addressed in the short term
  - contamination on less immediately dangerous sites should be dealt with only as and when those sites come up for redevelopment.

These policy parameters have been encapsulated in the new regime, though, as with any regime of such complexity, these ideas cause as many problems as they solve.

The Government's stated objectives for the new regime are:

- to identify and remove unacceptable risks to human health and the environment
- to seek to bring damaged land back into beneficial use
- to seek to ensure that the cost burdens faced by individuals, companies and society as a whole are proportionate, manageable and economically sustainable.

Recent policy pronouncements on the use of brownfield sites for 60 per cent of the new stock of housing required by 2016 have highlighted the overlaps between pollution control and planning law, and will continue to create tensions in the construction and property sectors for years to come.

How many contaminated sites are there in the UK? Estimates vary, and the UK Government itself refers to a figure of between 50,000 and 100,000 hectares; but on one interpretation of the new definition (see below) it could be argued that there are very few which actually pose any real threat, and the new legislation needs to be analysed closely to see if any particular site is indeed 'contaminated land'.

OUTLINE OF THE NEW REGIME

The new regime for contaminated land set out in the Environmental Protection Act 1990 (EPA 1990), Pt IIA, ss. 78A–78YC, came into force on 1 April 2000. The provisions of the Act are supplemented by the Contaminated Land (England) Regulations 2000 (CL(E)R 2000 (SI 2000 No. 227)), and Guidance Notes issued in the form of a DETR Circular on Contaminated Land ('Guidance'). All these documents need to be read together to get a full picture of the way the new rules are expected to work. The legislation, together with Annexes 3, 5 and 6 of the Guidance, is reproduced in Appendices 1 to 3 at the end of this book.

What do the new rules require? Primarily the task of making the new rules work will fall to local authorities, though some sites, because of their particular potential for harm, are to be designated as 'special' sites (CL(E)R 2000, reg. 2 and sch. 1) and these will be regulated by the Environment Agency. The procedure is the same, though, whoever is the regulator, and it entails the following stages.

Identifying a contaminated site

Contaminated land is defined by EPA 1990, s. 78A(2), as being:

> ... any land which appears to the local authority in whose area it is situated to be in such a condition, by reason of substances in, on or under land, that—
> (a)   significant harm is being caused or there is a significant possibility of such harm being caused; or
> (b)   pollution of controlled waters is being, or is likely to be, caused;
> and in determining whether any land appears to be such land, the local authority shall ... act in accordance with guidance issued by the Secretary of State ...

The Guidance requires a strategic approach, formulated over the first 15 months of the regime's operation, to any programme of land investigation, phased according to priority. On a specific site, the regulator is required to undertake a complex process of risk analysis, requiring the regulator to identify a contaminant, a receptor which is likely to be harmed by the contaminant should the two come into contact, and some plausible pathway by which the two could connect (for example, by airborne or subterranean migration). (See Guidance, Annex 3, Chapters A and B.) Even this is not sufficient, as the legislation requires that significant harm be caused, or may result, to the receptor.

The receptors recognised by the Guidance are limited to five categories only (humans, buildings, commercial crops, commercial livestock and certain types of ecosystem), and the types of harm are also limited as to what can qualify as 'significant' (Guidance, Annex 3, Chapter A, para. A.23, Table A). In the case of human receptors, for example, a disease will count as significant, but there will be debates over exactly what diseases will count.

Once all four requirements are met, there exists a 'significant pollutant linkage', or SPL; and where there is an SPL the authority must designate the site as contaminated (EPA 1990, ss. 78B(3) and 78E(1)).

Identifying the steps necessary to remediate the land

The enforcing authority must now decide what steps are necessary to cause the land to cease to be contaminated (EPA 1990, s. 78E). Again, the CL(E)R 2000 and Guidance must be followed in the specification of the steps to be carried out, by whom and when. Regulators must consider the costs and benefits of the works specified and consider the 'practicability, durability and effectiveness' of the works. The detail of the works must be specified in a Remediation Notice (EPA 1990, s. 78E(1), CL(E)R 2000, reg. 4; Guidance, Annex 3, Chapter C).

There may be debate over whether the steps are adequate or too extreme, or whether there are cheaper and more effective approaches to the problem. For instance, an authority may take the view that to solve the problem the land must be dug up and treated, either *in situ* or *ex situ*, or be taken away and disposed of as waste within the meaning of the 1990 Act. The landowner, on the other hand, may be able to argue that it would be an equally effective solution simply to remove the receptor, or sever the pathway, which approaches may be significantly cheaper — though admittedly more short-term.

Identifying those responsible for carrying out the works

The policy of the legislation is that the polluter should pay, and indeed the party liable to carry out the works specified in the Remediation Notice is the 'original polluter'. This is in turn defined as the person who 'caused or knowingly permitted the substances ... to be [present] ... on the land' (EPA 1990, s. 78F; CL(E)R 2000, reg. 4(1)(d)).

The main aim is that the person who caused the substances to be there in the first place should pay to remove them. This is logical and inoffensive. However, it is also possible that that someone can be classed as an 'original' polluter by having failed to remove something that was already on or in the land. It has been established by case law (see *Schulman's Incorporated* v *NRA* [1993] Env LR D1) that a person 'permits' something if he or she could have done something about it but failed to do so, and 'knows' of it if he or she had actual knowledge, or constructive knowledge borne of failing to make obvious enquiries or turning a blind eye to obvious risks. This starts to create obvious cause for concern and argument. There is a real risk that buyers of sites which could realistically be expected to have contamination on them (all but the greenest of greenfield sites) may be classed as the original polluters of the land if they fail to realise the risk of contamination and thereby fail to do anything to alleviate it. This is all the more likely the longer they are in possession of it. Thus current owners and purchasers can be made liable for historic pollution which they themselves did not initially cause. Further, if the current owner is the only person readily identifiable, he or she will bear all the cost of the remediation works (Guidance, Annex 3, Chapter D, Pt 5, para D.41(c)). In any event, if no 'original polluter' can be found, the current owner or occupier faces the remediation bill (EPA 1990, s. 78F(4)).

In order to try to alleviate some of the difficulties that this notion introduces, the Guidance contains complicated formulae by which parties may seek to be excluded from the categories of liable parties — if they have already effectively paid for the cost of remediation on a recent disposal of the site by taking a price cut, or if they have made a full revelation of the contamination to the buyer of the land before exchange of contracts — and there will be much litigation over whether and, if so, in what circumstances, these exceptions actually apply (Guidance, Annex 3, Chapter D, Pts 5 and 7). Rules also set out how costs are to be shared if there is more than one party responsible for the remediation (Guidance, Annex 3, Chapter D, Pts 6 and 8).

In addition, the Guidance sets out the circumstances in which someone who is potentially liable to pay some part of the cost of a clean-up can argue that he or she does not have the means to pay, and can thus be relieved of the obligation to pay. In such circumstances this 'orphan' liability has to be borne by the local authority (Guidance, Annex 3, Chapter E).

The whole regime is further complicated by the fact that there are some convoluted overlaps with other regimes of environmental control (Guidance, Annex 1, paras 45–71) which are only unhappily dealt with, and a system of appeals which provides 24 grounds on which to challenge a regulator's decisions (CL(E)R 2000, regs 7 to 12).

The prospect of litigation may make most regulators seek to sort out the problems on a voluntary basis, which is permissible under the legislation (EPA 1990, s. 78H(5)(b)). This is to be encouraged by the Government, which intends to bar anyone who is undertaking a clean-up under the force of a Remediation Notice from any landfill tax exemption, to which they will be entitled if doing the works voluntarily (Guidance, Annex 1, para. 71(c)).

There is to be a system of public registers which records designations, specified works, voluntary works undertaken and any appeals lodged, which should enable potential buyers of sites to get some idea of what they might find and thus what to ask in any purchase transaction. The registers will also record so-called remediation statements, which are lodged by the authorities if at any stage the full Remediation Notice procedure cannot be followed, perhaps because works would be too costly, no one can be found to foot the bill or those who can be found cannot afford to carry out the works (EPA 1990, ss. 78R–78T; CL(E)R 2000, reg. 16 and sch. 3). In such cases, there may be a blighting effect on the land, as it is registered as contaminated but there may have been difficulties cleaning it up. In any event, the register system provides no mechanism for any land to be given a clean bill of health even after a clean-up operation (EPA 1990, s. 78R(3); Guidance, Annex 2, paras 15.3–15.5), and this factor above all renders the scheme of little comfort to sellers and buyers alike. There is, however, an indication of how the regulator may 'sign off' a site on an informal basis (Guidance, Annex 2, para. 15.6).

Nevertheless, close inspection of such registers will be essential if buyers, developers, owners, tenants and mortgagees are to avoid an expensive future liability. *Caveat emptor* is still the guiding principle.

Chapter 2
The Definition of Contaminated Land

WHAT IS CONTAMINATED LAND?

How contaminated land is defined is the cornerstone of the operation of the legislation and the entirety of Government policy regarding pollution in the UK landmass. Too wide a definition will lead to much expense being wasted on land which is actually causing no real harm, whereas too restrictive a definition will result in harm going unregulated and unchecked.

The definition, or rather, the practical operation of it, is derived from the primary legislation and the associated Guidance notes on its implementation. Between them, they contrive to create a complex network of risk assessment principles which may be difficult to operate in practice.

'Contaminated land' is defined in EPA 1990, s. 78A(2) as being:

> ... any land which appears to the local authority in whose area it is situated to be in such a condition, by reason of substances in, on or under land, that—
> (a)   significant harm is being caused or there is a significant possibility of such harm being caused; or
> (b)   pollution of controlled waters is being, or is likely to be, caused;
> and in determining whether any land appears to be such land, the local authority shall ... act in accordance with guidance issued by the Secretary of State ...

The 'harm' referred to in s. 78A(2)(a) is defined by s. 78A(4) as meaning:

> ... harm to the health of living organisms or other interference with the ecological systems of which they form part and, in the case of man, includes harm to his property.

There are some features to note about this definition:

(a)   if there is no harm, land is not 'contaminated' within the meaning of the section, despite the presence of harmful matter; and

(b)   land is 'contaminated' only if the harm, or risk of harm, to the non-aquatic environment is significant; it is 'contaminated' if there is any risk of water pollution, however small.

Each regulating authority is under a duty to have regard to any Guidance issued by the DETR or the Environment Agency when assessing whether land in its area is contaminated. There is express provision within the Act for such Guidance to make provision for different weight to be attached to different descriptions of harm to health or property and other factors.

The definitions of 'harm' and 'significant' — and therefore the practical impact of the whole provision — are the subject of the Guidance. The Guidance stipulates that the definition of 'contaminated land' is to be interpreted in the following way:

(a)   'Harm' is to be regarded as significant only if it is of the following types:

(i)   death, disease, serious injury, genetic mutation, birth defects or impairment of reproductive function in humans (a 'human health effect'); this is further defined as including an 'unhealthy' condition of the body or part of it and can include, for example, cancer, liver dysfunction or extensive skin ailments, or even mental dysfunction attributable to some pollutant's effect on the body;

(ii)   irreversible adverse change in the functioning of an ecological system (or any species of special interest sustained by such a system) in a location protected under the Wildlife and Countryside Act 1981, European sites protected under reg. 10 of the Conservation Regulations 1994, sites afforded policy protection under para. 13 of Planning Policy Guidance Note 9 on nature conservation, or nature reserves established under the National Parks and Access to the Countryside Act 1949 (an 'ecological system effect');

(iii)   death, disease, other physical damage to livestock, crops, produce or domesticated or wild animals subject to hunting rights, amounting to 20 per cent or more of their value (an 'animal or crop effect'); and

(iv)   substantial damage to, or structural failure of buildings, or interference with rights of occupation, such that they can no longer be used for the intended purpose (a 'building effect').
(See Guidance, Annex 3, Chapter A, para. A.23, Table A.)

An authority must confine its identification of targets to those likely to be present due to the current use of the site only.

(b)   In assessing 'risk', authorities are to assess the possibility of harm, and its significance, by reference to:

(i)   the effects of the contamination; and
(ii)   fundamental principles of risk assessment.

Risk assessment involves an actual determination of the extent of contamination in a piece of land, i.e., the contaminants present and their concentration, their tendency to migrate, the geo-technical ground conditions in the locality (how might they contribute to the movement of the contaminant), the likely effects of an escape or migration and, in particular, how quickly harm may be suffered after exposure to the contaminant. The essence of the question for the authority is: how likely is it that an escape will actually occur, and what harm will follow if it does? (See Guidance, Annex 3, Chapter A, paras A.9–A.21.)

Substances, the routes by which they move and the entity which may be affected are described in terms of 'contaminant–pathway–receptor' (often referred to as 'source–pathway–target'), and when all three elements are present a 'pollutant linkage' exists. If significant harm is likely to result, a 'significant pollutant linkage' is present (Guidance, Annex 3, Chapter A, para. A.20).

In general, the more severe the harm, the greater its degree, the shorter the timescale for it to occur or the greater the vulnerability of the receptor, the more significant is the risk (Guidance, Annex 3, Chapter A, paras. A.27–A.34).

In determining the risk of water pollution, the authority is to ignore historic water pollution that is unlikely to recur. Only current or potential future water pollution can support a finding that the land is contaminated (Guidance, Annex 3, Chapter A, paras A.35–A.39).

The operation of the new regime is profoundly curtailed by the formulation of the new definition, and the guidance on how it is to be interpreted.

Only the receptors mentioned are recognised by the legislation, and all others are to be ignored by the authorities. One notable omission from the list is land itself — premises and buildings are recognised receptors but land itself is not. Subterranean migration of a contaminant from one site to another would not, of itself, give the recipient landowner any right to complain that his site is now contaminated under the new legislation (though he would have remedies in civil law). An authority would have to wait until a recognised receptor did emerge and then require the clean-up of that site giving rise to the problem. If this was the 'recipient' site, it would nevertheless be the polluter of the original site who would have to foot the bill. It seems, though, that the regime is not to be used to prevent the actual migration itself.

Likewise, the recognised types of harm are very narrow, and this limits the use of the new powers (intentionally, no doubt) to those sites which give rise to real and imminent risks to health.

However, the definitions do pose problems of their own. For instance, with regard to human health effects, is asthma a disease in the same league as cancer or liver dysfunction? If so, land giving rise to such an impact on health is contaminated; if not, it is not. Thus, whether land is contaminated is as much a product of medical debate as it is a product of chemistry or geology.

Land is contaminated if there is *any* risk of water pollution, however small, and this presents the authorities with a tension between the wording of the legislation and the ethos of the Guidance, which suggests that action be taken only in instances of real harm. This tension is due to the overlap with several provisions of the water legislation (see below), and while it may be overcome by recognising that although a site may be 'contaminated' by reason of minimal amounts of water pollution, the amount of clean-up required may be small or non-existent, it is still an uneasy situation. So much so that the Government is intending to review the wording of the principal legislation, though whether of the water legislation or of Pt IIA of the 1990 Act is unclear.

INTERACTION WITH OTHER LEGISLATIVE REGIMES

There are several other regimes which are intended to deal with many aspects of pollution and contamination and which could overlap with the operation of Pt IIA. They are:

- planning law
- radioactive substances legislation
- food safety
- health and safety
- major accident hazards
- landfill tax
- integrated pollution control/pollution prevention and control
- waste management
- statutory nuisances
- water pollution
- sewer discharges.

How are these overlaps resolved?

Planning law

Planning law is essentially focused on future land use, and all decisions regarding planning consent and conditions are taken with that future use in mind.

Contamination in the ground on any site coming up for redevelopment is a material consideration for the purposes of the planning legislation, and conditions will therefore be set by the planning authorities which take the implications of that contamination into account and which require its remediation as part of the development work. It will thus be the developer who has the task of remediating the contamination as part of the development and who must therefore take such costs into account in any purchasing decision.

Any such remediation will be policed via the planning system and not Pt IIA of the EPA 1990. Remediation under Pt IIA is intended to deal with current land use only.

Radioactive substances legislation

Radioactive substances and their effects are specifically removed from the normal ambit of Pt IIA, but the facility is retained for the Secretary of State to apply parts of it to radioactive contamination by regulation (EPA 1990, s. 78YC). A consultation process is currently underway on this topic.

Food safety

Authorities using Pt IIA powers are to liaise with the Food Standards Agency and MAFF over any use by the latter bodies of their powers of control under Part I of the Food and Environment Protection Act 1985.

Health and safety

Health and safety issues under the Health and Safety at Work Act 1974 may arise on any site where workers may be at risk of exposure to contaminants. In any such case authorities under Pt IIA of the EPA 1990 are to liaise with the Health and Safety Executive to ensure that no duplication of control takes place and that the most appropriate system of control is used to deal with the problem.

Major accident hazards

The Control of Major Accident Hazards Regulations 1999 require action plans in relation to dangerous substances stored on sites, providing for the steps to be taken in the event of an escape. Authorities under Pt IIA of the 1990 Act should again liaise with the Health and Safety Executive who oversee such plans.

Landfill tax

Landfill tax under the Finance Act 1996 will be payable on any wastes going to landfill. However, exemption is available for wastes from contaminated sites or those remediated as part of certain developments. This exemption will, however, *not* be available to anyone cleaning up a site as part of enforcement action under Pt IIA of the EPA 1990, though it will still be available to those cleaning up a site voluntarily (see Guidance, Annex 1, para. 71(c)). This is intended to be a fiscal incentive to voluntary clean-up.

Integrated pollution control/pollution prevention and control

Integrated pollution control (IPC) is a regulatory system of licensing for heavily polluting industrial processes. The IPC system contained in Pt I of the EPA 1990 comprises a power of clean-up, exercisable by the licensing authority in the event of any breach of a licence condition. The Act specifically provides that to the extent that any contaminant is already subject to control under Pt I, it cannot also constitute contaminated land under Pt IIA.

Pollution prevention and control (PPC) is a similar system, introduced by the Pollution Prevention and Control Act 1999 in response to a European Directive, which supersedes Pt I of the EPA 1990. Its essential components are identical though, and the 1999 Act also provides that to the extent that any contaminant is already subject to control under PPC, it cannot also constitute contaminated land under Pt IIA of EPA 1990.

IPC/PPC clean-up powers can be used to clean up land to any extent, and are not subject to the restrictive operative provisions of Pt IIA. Clean-up operations ordered under Pt IIA may constitute regulated processes under IPC/PPC.

Waste management

The waste management licensing regime contained in Pt II of the EPA 1990 deals with the operation of waste-related processes. To the extent that material is already liable to be dealt with under Pt II, it cannot also constitute contaminated land under Pt IIA (EPA 1990, s. 78YB(2)). However, any material removed as part of a remediation operation under Pt IIA may constitute waste (or even special waste), thus requiring a licence or other compliance procedures.

Statutory nuisances

Statutory nuisances under Pt III of the EPA 1990 are defined to include 'premises or accumulations' which could be a pollution or health risk, as well as the more routine examples such as smoke and noise. However, this would have meant that Pt III could have been used to require the abatement of any pollution risk arising on premises, which is exactly what the new regime in Pt IIA of the Act is supposed to address. Moreover, Pt III has been in force in one form or another for centuries and is familiar, quick and cheap.

In order to give Pt IIA a fighting chance, the legislation has been amended to provide that no land in a 'contaminated state' can now be a statutory nuisance (Environment Act 1995, sch. 22, para. 89). The definition of 'land in a contaminated state' includes any land on which contaminants are present and which may cause harm, and this is of course *not* the same as it being contaminated within the meaning of Pt IIA, which requires additional criteria to be met.

Thus one faces the situation where land may be in a contaminated state by virtue of the presence of chemicals on it, but is not yet so dangerous as to pose a real risk of significant harm to any recognised receptor. Such a site cannot be 'contaminated land', but neither can it now be a statutory nuisance. An authority is thus left powerless to deal with it.

It seems that this lacuna in the drafting of the legislation is intentional: it is Government policy — and now the law — that unless a site is imminently going to kill someone it should be left alone. Land is either 'contaminated' within the meaning of Pt IIA, or it is nothing. Deliberate this may be, desirable it is not.

Water pollution

Wherever and whenever water pollution occurs, however insignificant or harmless it may have been, the clean-up powers contained in the Water Resources Act 1991, ss. 161A–161D come into play. These enable the Environment Agency as water regulator to serve a works notice on those responsible for the water pollution requiring them to clean it, and all its consequences, up. Moreover, the notice can be used to prevent anticipated water pollution before it occurs.

There is a clear, and undesirable, overlap between these powers and those under Pt IIA of the EPA 1990, which can also be used whenever water pollution occurs. In any incident of water pollution, which set of powers should be used and by whom?

Logic would suggest that it should be the Water Resources Act powers that should be exercisable by the Agency — they are, after all, the water specialists. The 1990 Act would thus be left to deal with land-based contamination only. Sadly, logic has not guided Government thinking on this matter and the Guidance suggests that it should be the Pt IIA powers which should be used, the local authorities liaising with the Environment Agency over the terms and conditions to impose in dealing with any water pollution.

It remains to be seen what point there is in having the works notice powers in the 1991 Act, and the Government has indicated a desire to amend primary legislation to clarify this overlap, which is, for the time being, dealt with under an Environment Agency policy statement on the use of the works notice procedure. It seems that the latter is of use only if and when Pt IIA does not apply, but it is hard to envisage circumstances of water pollution emanating from land in which it would not.

Sewer discharges

Discharges of trade effluent to sewers are regulated under the Water Industry Act 1991. That piece of legislation contains no statutory powers of clean-up, and in that sense there is no overlap with the new regime in Pt IIA of the 1990 Act. However, it is just about conceivable that leakages into the sewerage system from a contaminated site may amount to an unlawful trade effluent discharge.

THE INSPECTION DUTY

The early months of the operation of the new regime will be taken up with the inspection duty, whereby the authorities must identify those sites in their areas which meet the definitional criteria for designation as 'contaminated'.

Here one must read the primary legislation in conjunction with the associated Regulations and Guidance notes issued in association with them to understand the whole picture.

Primary responsibility for identifying contaminated sites will rest with local authorities, i.e., the district council or unitary authority. They are obliged to inspect land in their area from time to time for the purpose of identifying contaminated land (EPA 1990, s. 78B), and such land as is liable for designation as a 'special site' (EPA 1990, s. 78C).

In the case of the latter category — sites which may be particularly hazardous — the local authority must refer the site to the Environment Agency for a decision on whether it should be designated as a 'special site'. If it is so designated, only the

Environment Agency has the power to determine when and how it should be remediated, and by whom (EPA 1990, s. 78A(9)).

When identifying sites, the enforcing authority is entitled to take into account the cumulative impact of two or more sites when assessing the 'significant harm' or 'pollution' (EPA 1990, s. 78X).

The CL(E)R 2000, reg. 2 and sch. 1 stipulate what sites are to be classed as 'special sites', and they include:

(a) land contaminated by waste acid tars, petroleum, oil, explosives, nuclear material, chemical weapons or toxins;

(b) land comprised in the Ministry of Defence Estate; and

(c) land used by visiting forces.

The authority is required to have a written strategy for the inspection process ensuring a consistent, ordered approach to the task of inspection, taking into account the information already in its possession and any additional matters brought to its attention by third parties (Guidance, Annex 3, Chapter B, Pts 3 and 4).

Authorities will have 15 months from the introduction of the new regime to formulate their inspection policies and strategies, though much of the groundwork for this has already been undertaken by many authorities as they had prepared for the introduction of the contaminated land registers in 1990, which were later abandoned in favour of the EPA 1990, Pt IIA.

Any attempts to gain information from authorities about their policies, strategies or views as to which sites may fall within the definition of 'contaminated land' will be met with a refusal on the grounds that the investigations are incomplete — a justification for withholding information under the Freedom of Access to Environmental Information Regulations 1992 (SI 1992 No. 3240) (see also *Maile v Wigan Metropolitan Borough Council*, May 1999 (unreported, but see ENDS Report 294, July 1999, p. 55)).

Specifically, the authority is required to have established the reasonable possibility of a pollutant linkage — the presence of a receptor, a contaminant and a plausible pathway — before undertaking any intrusive ground investigations. It is required to obtain 'sufficient information' to enable it to form a judgment as to the extent of contamination. The authority need not produce a complete characterisation of the nature of the contamination, but only as much as is sufficient for it to make the determination that land is contaminated (Guidance, Annex 3, Chapter B, Pt 3, paras B.18–B.25).

In making the determination, the authority is required to indicate the basis on which the designation is made (significant harm being caused, risk of water pollution, etc.) and to specify what pollutant linkage gives rise to the designation of land as 'contaminated' (Guidance, Annex 3, Chapter B, Pt 3, paras B.39–B.51).

Land shall not be regarded as contaminated in relation to water pollution risks unless consultation with the Environment Agency has been carried out, or if (*inter alia*) risk management arrangements are already in place to prevent such pollution (Guidance, Annex 3, Chapter B, Pt 3, para. B.51).

IDENTIFICATION AND DESIGNATION OF SITES

The authority is obliged to carry out inspections of its area from time to time in accordance with its strategic plan. It must seek to identify those areas of land within its jurisdiction which meet the statutory definition as set out in the Act and refined in the Guidance Notes.

Once the authority identifies such a site it must then give notice of that fact to all concerned parties (EPA 1990, s. 78B(3)) and it is at this point that it can then be said that the site has been designated as contaminated.

This designation is a positive obligation, not a discretion, and the authority will be aware that only by officially designating the site will it have any powers to deal with it. Moreover, local concerns and the vigilance of public interest groups may exert a certain pressure on an authority to make the designation for fear of judicial review of its decision. Once made, however, the designation carries with it certain obligations and implications. It will now become compulsory to serve a remediation notice in respect of the land (EPA 1990, s. 78E) and to maintain details on official registers (EPA 1990, s. 78R).

The regulatory machinery has now been engaged.

Chapter 3
Remediation Works

INTRODUCTION

Once a site has been formally identified as contaminated, the authority must then serve a remediation notice on those responsible, requiring them to clean it up or otherwise to undertake such works as are necessary to cause the land to cease to be contaminated.

The steps set out in the remediation notice are the 'remediation works', which must be carried out by the responsible party, known as the 'appropriate person'.

Under the EPA 1990, s. 78A(7), the definition of 'remediation' includes:

(a)   an assessment of the condition of land;

(b)   the doing of any works, carrying out of any operations or taking of any steps in relation to any land or waters for preventing, minimising, remedying or mitigating the effects of significant harm or pollution;

(c)   the restoration of land or waters to their former state; and

(d)   inspections from 'time to time'.

In specifying the steps required under a remediation notice the authority can only require reasonable steps to be taken having regard to the costs of carrying out the work and the seriousness of the harm/pollution caused (EPA 1990, s. 78E(4) and (5)).

The precise requirements with regard to the content of remediation notices and the procedures to be followed are dealt with by way of Regulations (EPA 1990, s. 78E(6)). In addition, enforcing authorities are obliged to take into account any guidance from the Secretary of State in relation to what is to be done, the standard to which it must be carried out and the definition of 'reasonable' in the context of the cost–benefit analysis (EPA 1990, s. 78E(5)).

The CL(E)R 2000, reg. 4, provides that the following information must be contained in a remediation notice (see further below). This includes:

(a)   the capacity in which the authority believes the person served to be an appropriate person;

(b)   details of the SPL giving rise to the designation of the land as contaminated; and

(c)   details of the works to be carried out, by whom and in what shares and proportions.

The Guidance differentiates between a number of terms (Annex 3, Chapter C, Pt 2, para. C.8):

(a)   a remediation action is a single action to be taken in respect of a pollutant linkage;

(b)   a remediation package is a full set of actions appropriate to a pollution linkage; and

(c)   a remediation scheme is the full set of actions or packages appropriate to a specific area of contamination.

The remediation notice must specify in detail the works, actions, packages or schemes the authority thinks necessary to achieve the objective of causing the land to cease to be contaminated (see further below). These may be required to be effected immediately, or may be phased.

SPECIFICATION OF WORKS

The Guidance sets out the meaning of the term 'remediation', and the standard to which such works should be carried out (see Annex 3, Chapter C, Pts 3 and 4). The overall approach is that remediation should be undertaken only to the standard required to make the land suitable for use, though voluntary clean-up to a higher standard is always possible. The works specified in the notice may require not only a clean-up of the site, but also assessment measures and monitoring works (Guidance, Annex 3, Chapter C, Pt 7).

The Guidance emphasises that the packages of works required should amount to the best practicable techniques of remediation to remove or treat the pollutant, break or remove the pathway or protect or remove the receptor. Best practicable techniques are to be judged by reference to the optimum combination of the qualities of reasonableness (on a cost–benefit analysis), practicability, effectiveness and durability. The crucial question is what constitutes the remediation work that is 'best' suited to all these competing factors. The Guidance suggests that the remediation works specified should be such as to enable the identified pollutant linkage which led to the original designation to cease to exist. This may mean simply severing the pathway (e.g., by tarmacadaming a surface), or removing a receptor from the area of danger (e.g., by fencing it off) rather than by cleaning the subsoil (Guidance, Annex 3, Chapter C, Pt 4, paras C.17–C.28).

Such simple strategies may be the 'best' in the circumstances, but are necessarily short-term and may not be effective in perpetuity. Dealing with one sort of linkage in this way does not mean that another different sort may not spring up elsewhere, requiring another notice and more works. It means that land is never given a clean bill of health as it may be redesignated as contaminated at a later stage should a new receptor or pathway emerge. In addition, this semantic approach to the problem may not satisfy local communities who see clean-up as something more fundamental. However, this short-termism is entirely in accord with Government policy, which is to leave the long-term, heavyweight solutions until such time as the land comes up for redevelopment when planning conditions can be used to require developers to carry out the necessary engineering works.

The Guidance also sets out the considerations as to the reasonableness, practicability, effectiveness and durability of the remediation in deciding what works the authority may legitimately require (Annex 3, Chapter C, Pts 5 and 6). 'Reasonableness' involves the authority deciding what strategies are acceptable given the cost involved (including actual costs, disruption costs and future maintenance costs) as measured against the seriousness of the harm (type of receptor, actual damage caused and irreversibility) and the likely benefit to be produced by undertaking them. For example, requiring full-blown clean-up now may not be sensible if, in the near future, a similar aim could be achieved more cheaply using newer technology. The financial means of the liable party are not relevant to the question of what steps can be required — a defence of poverty is not available at this stage in the process.

One complication for the authority is that any remediation notice must show how these competing considerations have been applied by the authority — not only what its decision is, but how it came to make it. This would seem to amplify the opportunity for challenging a notice.

'Practicability' involves determining what works are logistically possible, given the location, the technology available, the time-frame and any regulatory difficulties regarding health and safety or consent conditions. Moreover, the detrimental effect of the doing of the works themselves must not be ignored.

'Effectiveness' is to be judged not only by reference to the immediate effects of an action, but also by its longer-term effect.

'Durability' is to be judged by reference to the length of time the pollutant linkage is likely to remain a risk of harm. Clearly, if a linkage is likely to remain a risk for 10 years, the remediation works should be designed to last at least that long. Any shorter period of durability will require the same linkage to be re-treated within the life-span of the pollution problem itself, which is undesirably repetitive. If this is unavoidable, regular monitoring and maintenance may be required.

Remediation steps cannot be required for any purposes other than those set out in the Guidance, and, in particular, are referable to current land use only.

WHEN WORKS CANNOT BE REQUIRED

There are a number of circumstances in which the duty to serve a remediation notice does not apply. A remediation notice *must not* be served where:

(a) the enforcing authority is satisfied that a site is contaminated but no remediation works can be specified to be carried out because they would be unreasonably expensive (EPA 1990, s. 78H(5)). In such circumstances it must publish a remediation statement setting out the grounds for taking the view that remediation works cannot be specified (EPA 1990, s. 78H(6));

  (b) the authority is satisfied that appropriate steps are being, or will be taken without the service of a notice (EPA 1990, s. 78H(5)). In such circumstances, the person who would have received the notice is required to prepare, within a reasonable period, a remediation statement setting out what works will be carried out, and within what period (EPA 1990, s. 78H(7));

  (c) the authority itself would be the recipient (EPA 1990, s. 78H(5)); or

  (d) grounds already exist for the exercise by the authority of its own clean-up powers in respect of the site (EPA 1990, s. 78H(5)).

These exceptions do not apply where there is imminent danger of serious harm or serious pollution of controlled waters (EPA 1990, s. 78H(4)).

A further restriction is placed upon the authority in that it cannot issue a notice where powers are available to the Environment Agency under the EPA 1990, s. 27 in relation to remediation of pollution caused by prescribed processes (EPA 1990, s. 78YB). This will be amended to reflect the introduction of the PPC regime under the Pollution Prevention and Control Act 1999.

ACCESS TO SITES TO CARRY OUT WORKS

A remediation notice can require an appropriate person to carry out works which he or she is not otherwise entitled to do, because, for example, he or she is no longer in possession of the site and has no rights of access to it (EPA 1990, s. 78G(1)). In these circumstances, the owner or occupier of land has a statutory obligation to allow remediation works to be carried out on land or waters which he or she owns or occupies (EPA 1990, s. 78G(2)).

Before the remediation notice is served the enforcing authority has to use its reasonable endeavours to consult with all those parties who might be required to grant rights to the party carrying out the remediation works, though this requirement does not apply where there is imminent danger of serious harm etc. (EPA 1990, s. 78G(3), (4)). No provision is made in the Act for forcing or expediting the consent of those parties should they refuse.

Where rights are granted, compensation will be payable by the appropriate person (EPA 1990, s. 78G(5)). The cost of compensation could, of course, be greater than that of carrying out the remediation works themselves. The CL(E)R 2000, reg. 6 and sch. 2 provide the formula for assessing compensation, and the procedure to be followed. Broadly, this mirrors the regime in the Land Compensation Act 1961. The Guidance provides that the cost of compensating the occupier for rights of access is to be one of the costs to be identified by the authority in, and borne by the appropriate person receiving, the remediation notice (Annex 3, Chapter C, para. C.35).

REMEDIATION NOTICES

Once a site has been identified as contaminated land (or a special site), the relevant authority is under a duty to prepare a 'remediation notice' specifying what must be done by way of remediation (EPA 1990, s. 78E). There are certain circumstances in which a remediation notice cannot and must not be served (see p. 17 above).

The CL(E)R 2000, reg. 4, stipulates the information to be contained in a remediation notice. This includes:

- relevant names and addresses
- the locations of the pollutant linkages
- dates
- an identification of the reasons for the designation of the site as contaminated land
- an identification of the appropriate persons and reasons for their selection
- the works required (see p. 16 above) and time limit for completion
- evidence of the application by the authority of all and any relevant guidance
- that offences of non-compliance may be committed and penalties
- rights in relation to appeals.

There is so much information to be included that remediation notices are likely to be complex and lengthy documents; and if any information is missing or inaccurate, the notice will be invalid.

A scrupulous examination of any notice served would almost inevitably produce grounds for challenge to the form and content of the notice, or the processes of decision-making revealed by it. The grounds of appeal specifically refer to the adequacy of the notice as being one justification for complaint (see p. 33 below).

REGULATORS' POWERS TO CARRY OUT WORKS

Although the intention is that the appropriate person will carry out all the necessary works, there are nevertheless residual powers vested in the authorities to carry out the works themselves in certain circumstances.

Under the EPA 1990, s. 78N, the relevant authority has the power to carry out remediation works itself:

(a)   where it is necessary to prevent imminent serious harm being caused;

(b)   where any requirement of a remediation notice is not complied with;

(c)   where it is agreed that the authority should carry out the works;

(d)   where a remediation notice could not have specified works of the type required;

(e)   where the local authority would not be seeking to recover the costs from anyone else;

(f)   where there is no appropriate person on whom to serve a remediation notice (a so-called 'orphan' liability).

If works are carried out pursuant to either of the first two powers mentioned, the authority can recover the reasonable costs of the work (or at least a proportion of them) from the appropriate person, subject to guidance and any hardship caused (EPA 1990, s. 78P; see p. 30 below). Costs may include interest if the appropriate person is both the original polluter and the current owner of the contaminated land (EPA 1990, s. 78P(4)).

The relevant authority also has the power to serve a charging notice on the owner, which will constitute a charge on the premises which consist of or include the contaminated land in question. The costs of any charge may be paid by instalments over a maximum 30-year period (EPA 1990, s. 78P(5)-(13)). A person served with the charging notice has a right of appeal which must be made to the county court within 21 days of the receipt of the notice (EPA 1990, s. 78P(8)).

VOLUNTARY WORKS

Notwithstanding anything which is required to be carried out by a remediation notice, it is always open to an appropriate person to carry out works on a voluntary basis. Such an approach would have the following advantages:

(a)   The works — their specification and implementation — are under the control of the person carrying out the works rather than the authority (though the authority would need to approve the works).

(b)   It may be a cheaper strategy than the authority may have conceived.

(c)   It may deal with wider and more long-term issues than an authority has power to address.

(d)   No remediation notice can be served so long as the appropriate person intends to carry out such works (so no such notice appears on the public registers: EPA 1990, s. 78H(5)(b)).

(e)   The person carrying out the works can still claim landfill tax exemption.

(f)   Details of the works (though no guarantee of their effectiveness) will be recorded on the public registers (EPA 1990, s. 78R).

OFFENCES AND PENALTIES

Under the EPA 1990, s. 78M, it is an offence to fail to comply with a remediation notice without reasonable excuse. The offence can be tried only in the magistrates' court.

Where the contaminated land comprises industrial, trade or business premises, the maximum penalty is a fine of £20,000 with a further daily fine of up to £2,000 for every day before the enforcing authority begins to carry out any remediation. In cases of other contaminated land, the maximum fine is £5,000 with a maximum daily fine of £500 (10 per cent of Level 5) for every day before the enforcing authority begins to carry out any remediation.

Chapter 4
Who Pays for Remediation?

IDENTIFICATION OF LIABLE PARTIES

Government policy is that the polluter should pay. All or any of the (possibly several) persons who have contributed to the pollution should bear the cost of resolving the problems to which it has given rise.

Formulating the system to catch all those who should legitimately be caught — and to relieve those of liability who should be relieved — has been the most difficult aspect of the entire project. It has always been the Government's intention to avoid the American experience where, under the Superfund legislation, it is said, the litigation over the identification of liable parties has cost some 10 times as much as the actual clean-ups. Whether the UK will avoid the same fate is debatable, as the UK system is still fraught with difficulties, ambiguities and pitfalls.

Under the EPA 1990, s. 78F, there are three parties who may become potential recipients of remediation notices:

(a) the person(s) who caused or knowingly permitted the contaminating substances to be in, on or under the land in question (to be referred to as the 'original polluter');
(b) the owner for the time being of the contaminated land; and
(c) the occupier for the time being of the contaminated land.

This is largely consistent with the 'polluter pays principle', but has a number of defects in practice, not least of which is the fact that owners will get the bill if no one else can be found.

ORIGINAL POLLUTERS

The first, and most obvious, candidate for service of the remediation notice is the original polluter of the site. If you put the contaminant there in the first place, you should pay to take it away again. This has the advantage of simplicity, and the disadvantage of over-simplification, of course, as the identity of the original polluter may be complicated by a long history of contamination on the site.

Having found a likely polluter, or a number of likely polluters, the primary issue is whether they come into the category of 'causing' or 'knowingly permitting' the material to be present in, on or under the land. By analogy with a long line of criminal law authorities interpreting the same form of words (see, e.g., *Alphacell* v *Woodward* [1972] AC 824; *Empress Car Co. (Abertillery) Ltd* v *NRA* [1998] 2 WLR 350), the concept of 'causing' pollution will only require proof of some connection, however direct or indirect, between the activities of the polluter and the polluting emission into the ground — dumping, burying, leaking, over-filling, operating inefficiently, breaching bund walls, hosing excess chemicals down broken drains and the like. Simply carrying on the activity which caused the pollution is enough. It is not necessary to prove knowledge, negligence or fault. As long as the activity was itself intentional, all that is needed is a causal link between the activity and the pollution. Being part of the cause is enough (see *Attorney-General's Reference (No. 1 of 1994)* [1995] 2 All ER 1007). This formulation would be sufficiently wide to catch anyone who owned or operated the site and during whose tenure the substances came to be in the ground.

However, the definition of 'original polluter' goes further, and here the problems start to set in, as the definition also catches those who 'knowingly permit' the pollution to remain on the site.

'Permitting' the pollution can consist of merely allowing pollution to occur, i.e., not preventing it if it was possible to do so. It also covers allowing pollution to remain on a site, even if it was already there when the site was bought. Failing to remove such pollution may make a person liable as the original polluter of the site. Legally this may be acceptable, but it offends any lay notions of what it means to be a polluter.

The 'offence' is that of 'knowingly' permitting, and this gives rise to the question — what degree of knowledge is required? There is some authority for the view that, in addition to actual knowledge of the circumstances, turning a blind eye to the obvious or deliberately refraining from enquiry for fear of the truth, may attract liability (see *Schulman's Incorporated* v *NRA* [1993] Env LR D1). If a site owner or purchaser could have found out about the contamination (for example, by survey or investigation), could have done something to stop or remove it and failed to take those steps, he or she may be said to have 'knowingly permitted' it, and thus become liable as 'original polluter' to receive a remediation notice.

Assurances in the Guidance (Annex 2, paras 9.8-9.15) suggest that a person cannot be fixed with knowledge of the presence of contamination merely by the action of a local authority in investigating the site under Pt IIA of the 1990 Act. Such assurances, however, fail to deal with the issue of constructive knowledge having arisen by dint of a purchaser's failure to make reasonable enquiries at purchase, or during his or her own occupation. Despite requests to do so, the Government has signally failed to give any assurances that no liability will attach in such cases, and it must be assumed that it is the intention that successive owners may all be included in the category of 'original polluter' along with the person who first contaminated the land. This is less 'the polluter paying' and more 'the liability runs with the land'. This is all the more true when one takes into consideration the possibility that everyone bar the current owner may have either disappeared or become insolvent.

A cynic might suggest that the main purpose of all this legislative invention is to sensitise buyers to the possibility of contamination so they do not pay too much for a polluted site in the first place, leaving enough in their budget to pay for its clean-up. The doctrine of *caveat emptor* — and its younger relative 'let the buyer be well-informed about the possibility of liability' — is alive, well and living on a brownfield site near you.

OWNERS AND OCCUPIERS

Although primary responsibility for remediation rests with the person who caused or knowingly permitted the substance to be present in land (the 'original polluter', see above), who may in certain circumstances not even be the original polluter on the ambiguous wording of the Act, there is a residual responsibility which falls upon owners and occupiers of land.

Where, after reasonable inquiry, the original polluter cannot be 'found', the owner or the occupier for the time being becomes the appropriate person (EPA 1990, s. 78F(4)). 'Owner' is defined in s. 78A(9) as being the person who is or would be entitled to receive the rent for the property (other than a mortgagee not in possession). There is no statutory definition of 'occupier'. It will likely be taken to be the literal definition of someone in physical occupation of, or having some presence on, the land in question.

No formal guidance has been given in respect of the definition of 'reasonable inquiry', but the DETR policy is to let the courts determine the ambit of the phrase (Guidance, Annex 2, para. 9.19). There is also no formal guidance on the meaning of the word 'found'. The DETR view is that it means 'identified, in existence and located' (Annex 2, para. 9.17).

The liability of owners and occupiers is restricted with regard to remediation works in relation to the pollution of controlled waters. Where a party finds himself or herself responsible for remediation works solely as a result of his or her ownership or occupation of land (as opposed to being the original polluter), he or she will not be liable for any works relating to the pollution of controlled waters (EPA 1990, s. 78J).

The combination of these provisions means that it is in the owner's or occupier's interests to help the local authority to find the parties who are likely to be defined as the original polluters, as to do so would mean that the owner or occupier could no longer be served with the remediation notice. It would be useful, on any purchase transaction, to investigate the identity and whereabouts of previous owners and occupiers should the local authority have any difficulty tracking them down.

ESCAPES OF SUBSTANCES TO OTHER LAND

As contamination does not necessarily confine itself to boundaries of ownership or occupation, there is provision for the service of remediation notices where substances have escaped from their original resting place onto other land. The basic principle is that the original polluter of the first site (land A) is to be treated as the original polluter of any other land (land B, C etc.) to which the substance migrates (EPA 1990, s. 78K(1)).

Owners and occupiers of lands A, B or C are not liable to carry out remediation works in respect of contaminating substances unless the original polluter cannot be found, and in any event could then only be made liable to clean up land within their ownership or occupation (EPA 1990, s. 78K(3), (4)).

NON-LIABLE PARTIES

After much early debate, wherein the banks and other lenders were concerned that they could be made liable for the contaminating activities of those to whom they had lent money — and that they were being looked upon as the deep pocket — the 1990 Act specifically exempts certain persons from the category of potential 'appropriate persons'. They are referred to as 'persons acting in a relevant capacity' (EPA 1990, s. 78X(3)). This includes:

(a)   licensed insolvency practitioners;
(b)   the Official Receiver acting as a licensed insolvency practitioner;
(c)   the Official Receiver acting as a receiver or manager;
(d)   a receiver appointed by statute/court order (EPA 1990, s. 78X(4)).

In respect of clean-up costs, liability can be avoided by such persons except where the contamination is present as a result of any act done or omission made by the relevant person which it was unreasonable for a person acting in that capacity to do or make.

There is no guidance on the concept of 'reasonable behaviour', but merely carrying on a business pending re-sale is unlikely to attach liability to a licensed insolvency practitioner. Blatant, indeed negligent, disregard of contamination or deliberate dumping of material to make a site seem more attractive as a saleable item could still give rise to liability.

Criminal liability is not imposed unless there is a failure to comply with a requirement to do something for which the licensed insolvency practitioner is personally liable as a result of his unreasonable behaviour.

It should be noted that ordinary receivers appointed under a debenture or other security who are not licensed insolvency practitioners would not be covered by this exemption.

It is also interesting to note that lenders are not exempted wholesale in the same way. Lenders, or rather mortgagees, not in possession are exempted from the definition of 'owners', but it is still technically possible for a lender to be classified as an 'original polluter' if it causes or knowingly permits contamination. It is thus still possible for a lender to be made liable for the contaminating activities of a borrower.

EXCLUSION FROM LIABILITY

It is in the vexed area of exclusion from liability that the real meat of the new regime lies. Having identified a number of potential 'appropriate persons', the authority has to decide:

(a)   who is liable for what pollution;
(b)   if more than one person is liable for the same pollution, whether any of them should be relieved of liability altogether (the process of 'exclusion'); and
(c)   between those who remain, how the cost should be shared (apportionment).

Multiple sites of contamination, with separate appropriate persons

Different and separate remediation notices can require different things to be done by way of remediation by different appropriate persons in respect of different substances on the same site, or even the same substance in discrete locations where the separate depositors of the two 'lumps' of substance can be identified (EPA 1990, s. 78E(2)). Each appropriate person may, however, be served with a notice only in connection with any remediation which is 'to any extent referable' to substances caused or knowingly permitted by that party (EPA 1990, s. 78F(3)).

Single site of contamination, with multiple appropriate persons

Where the same remediation activity is required from different parties in respect of the same problem, the authority must first allocate responsibility for remediation to those persons who are potential appropriate persons, and then apportion the relative share of the cost of remediation to be borne by each. The questions to be determined by the authority are, respectively, (i) who is going to share the blame, and (ii) in what proportions?

In determining both these questions the authority must first decide whether anyone can be excluded from the 'liability group' (EPA 1990, s. 78F(6)), and then decide on the share to be borne by those who remain (EPA 1990, s. 78F(7)). The remediation notice must state the relative shares to be borne (EPA 1990, s. 78E(3)).

In this pursuit, regard must be had to the Guidance, which sets out in Annex 3, Chapter D, a series of principles on the basis of which certain persons and categories of persons can be excluded from the definition of 'appropriate persons' (exclusion), and costs can be shared between those who remain (apportionment: see further below).

The Guidance states that the first step is to define the 'liability group', i.e., all those who may be appropriate persons by the application of the definition in the Act. That means all those who caused or knowingly permitted the contaminants to be present in the land (original polluters). This class is called 'Class A appropriate persons'. The authority must also seek to identify all those who are owners and occupiers, liable as such because the original polluter cannot be found. This class is called 'Class B appropriate persons'.

The exclusion tests

The next step is to exclude from those groups anyone satisfying any one of a number of tests set out in the Guidance (see Annex 3, Chapter D, Pts 5 and 7). These tests are to be applied in the order set out in the Guidance.

The application of the exclusionary tests must stop if ever there is only one person left in the class, or must not be applied if applying any such test would have the effect of removing everyone from the class.

Only those who are not excluded by the operation of the tests are liable to receive the remediation notice.

The exclusion tests for Class A persons (original polluters)

Test 1	excludes anyone who is in the Class A group solely by reason of undertaking certain activities, such as (*inter alia*) lending to, insuring, advising, licensing, consenting to the activities of or leasing land to any other member of the liability group (paras D.47–D.50)
Test 2	excludes anyone who makes a relevant payment for remediation of land and that remediation is not carried out properly or at all (paras D.51–D.56)
Test 3	excludes anyone who has sold land on arms' length terms having provided sufficient information to the buyer to enable him or her to be aware of the pollution risk which has led to the designation (paras D.57–D.61)
Test 4	excludes anyone who deposits a substance A, which is, on its own, inert and of no risk, but which, when combined with substance B, becomes a pollutant (in this case the depositor of substance B becomes liable) (paras D.62–D.64)
Test 5	excludes anyone who deposits a substance which will not escape without intervention, but which later escapes due to intervention (in this case it is the intervener who is liable) (paras D.65–D.67)
Test 6	excludes anyone who deposits a substance which is not a risk due to the lack of a pathway or a receptor, but which later becomes a risk due to the subsequent introduction of a pathway or receptor (in this case it is the introducer of the pathway or receptor who is liable) (paras D.68–D.72).

Exclusion of members of a Class B liability group (owners and occupiers)

Test (a)	excludes anyone occupying the land under a licence with no marketable value
Test (b)	excludes anyone paying rent for the land and having no beneficial interest in the ownership of it other than the tenancy itself (para. D. 89).

In all cases, where the parties who are liable to have to share a clean-up liability choose to do so, they can agree between themselves how they are to share that cost, and the authorities must honour that agreement, and not apply the exclusionary tests.

Practical application of the exclusion tests

These exclusion tests may seem fine in isolation, and the intention of removing from liability those who have no real connection with the contamination is laudable, but the practicalities of the system lead to several areas of concern.

Test 1

This excludes those who are generally thought of as peripheral to the contaminating activity — advisers, lenders, landlords, surveyors and the like. Clearly those who are offering services to a polluting business would not imagine that they could be made liable for the effects of the polluting business's activities themselves. However, the fact that the exception exists at all indicates that in the Government's view it is at least theoretically possible that such peripheral service providers could be held at least to have permitted the activities in some way. If so, they are given an immediate exemption from liability, but the exemption can only operate at all if there are others who will be left in the Class A category after its operation. If there are no others then the lender or the adviser can be made to pay the clean-up bill.

Test 2

This excludes those who have, in some sense, already paid for the cost of a clean-up operation on the site and in relation to the pollution which is now giving rise to the problem. Having paid once, they will not be required to pay again, and this test gives the necessary exemption. Note, though, that to benefit from the exemption, the payment must have been made expressly for the purpose of the relevant clean-up, and must have been of an adequate size to pay for that clean-up. Moreover, the clean-up must not have been carried out properly or at all. The size and purpose of the payment must be specifically set out in the contract under the terms of which the payment has come to be made.

That said, the payment could take a number of forms and still qualify. It could be a specific payment made voluntarily or under court order, or, more likely, could take the form of a price reduction on a change of ownership of property, recorded fully and specifically in the contract. Properly evidenced price reductions thus remove a seller from the Class A category. General price reductions, not specifically evidenced in the agreement, do not.

Test 3

This excludes anyone who sells land to another member of the Class A group and who ensures that the purchaser had sufficient information about the nature and extent of the contamination to enable him or her to decide whether to proceed and, if so, with what price adjustments.

This is clearly an inducement to full disclosure on the part of the seller, and enables a buyer to make an informed choice on the purchase — knowing that if he or she proceeds it will be at his or her own risk as to the cost of the clean-up, as the seller will be excluded from the class.

The difficulty with this exclusion test is in the detail. Paragraph D.59 states that the sort of transaction to which the test applies is not confined to property deals pure and simple, but can involve any network of transactions as part of which property changes hands — a company share or business acquisition being the obvious other instance. Moreover, it states that in transactions between large commercial organisations (however they are to be defined), the mere offering of facilities for inspection, survey or investigation will be sufficient to fix the purchaser with all the knowledge he or she could have discovered had he or she undertaken such an investigation, whether he or she did or did not do so. This counts as full disclosure by the seller.

In addition, it should be noted that this aspect of the test is made retrospective and will catch any transaction entered into since 1990 (see para. D.59(d)). This may cause considerable upset and dislocation as such transactions may not have made sufficient provision for indemnity, and recent purchasers may have to bear the full clean-up costs alone.

Tests 4–6

These tests exclude the original polluter of the site in any circumstances where the pollutant linkage is attributable to the intervention of some other factor, without which there would have been no problem.

The Guidance seems to alter the operation of the Act on this point. It provides (see Test 6, paras D.68–D.72) that if the migration of the contamination would not have occurred without the act or omission of some third party, it is the third party intervener who is the appropriate person for service of the notice, rather than the original depositor of the substance. The Guidance proceeds on the basis that the third party intervener must also be in the liability group to start with, i.e., they must themselves be said to have caused or knowingly permitted the substance to be present, so as between co-polluters, it is the person who causes the migration rather than the original pollution who has to remediate.

The Act proceeds on the assumption that once a person deposits a substance, he or she is liable for everything and anything which subsequently happens to it. For the Guidance to change the express terms of the Act is a constitutional novelty, and it remains to be seen how the courts will interpret these provisions.

Tests (a) and (b)

These simply operate to exclude from liability those who only have a short-term interest in the land, leaving those with the long-term interest to bear the clean-up cost.

APPORTIONMENT OF LIABILITY

Having excluded persons from the liability group, it remains for the authority to apportion liability amongst those who remain.

As far as Class A persons are concerned, the Guidance suggests the following factors as being relevant to the determination of the proportion of costs to be borne by each member of the group (see Annex 3, Chapter D, Pt 6):

● relative degree of responsibility for the pollutant linkage
● whether they caused, or merely permitted the presence of the contaminant
● periods of ownership
● quantities of contaminant
● area of land owned
● opportunity to remove the contaminant.

The natural assumption would be that the original polluter of the site ('original' in the lay sense of being the person who caused the substances to be there in the first place) would have to bear the lion's share of the cost of clean-up. However, it is clear that it is quite possible for a subsequent owner to have to carry a heavier share, on the basis that he or she may have had more opportunity to correct the problem since it emerged, and the contamination issue is due to that person's indolence as much as to any other cause.

Companies and their officers are to be treated as one and the same entity for the purpose of apportionment.

As far as Class B persons are concerned, costs are to be shared in the proportions in which the owners or occupiers share the capital value of the land.

Though there is some discussion of the relative priority of these factors, it is by no means clear how they are to operate or what the outcome may be. Presumably, an authority would have to indicate how it had operated the principles in any case of dispute.

In order to allow the parties to a transaction the power to introduce some certainty into their own arrangements, the Guidance provides that where two or more appropriate persons have entered into an agreement on the division of liability for a pollutant linkage, the authority must honour that agreement (Annex 3, Chapter D, Pt 4, para. D.38). This will not occur, however, if the result of the agreement would be to place a financial burden on a party who would otherwise have been able to benefit from any restrictions on cost recovery (see below); in other words, if the authority is likely, indirectly, to have to shoulder more of the cost than it would otherwise have done, it can ignore the agreement altogether (para D.39). Whereas this makes sense in allowing an authority to disregard obvious attempts at avoidance, it could also have the effect that the parties legitimately enter into an agreement on liabilities which is later treated as worthless by the authority.

Any such contract would need to include indemnity clauses to restore the position intended to be achieved if the authority is entitled to and does ignore the agreement.

COST RECOVERY

Whenever a remediation notice is served, the expectation is that the recipient will undertake the clean-up at his or her expense. What happens if there is no one on whom the authority can legitimately serve a remediation notice? What if those who receive a notice fail to comply with it?

The 1990 Act provides for a number of circumstances in which an authority can exercise its powers of clean-up. In any such case, the authority will have borne the cost of the clean-up itself. It can then seek to recover those costs from any of those who should themselves have borne the cost. The only real defence to such a recovery claim is that of hardship (EPA 1990, s. 78P(2)).

The Guidance (Annex 2, paras 10.8–10.10) suggests that 'hardship' should be given its usual dictionary meaning of 'hardness of fate or circumstance, severe suffering or privation', and should be interpreted to include injustice, suffering and anxiety as well as financial impact. Authorities are encouraged to develop their own policies on cost recovery along other parameters — for example, whether the person served would be financially eligible to receive housing renovation grant (see Housing Renewal Grants Regulations 1996 (SI 1996 No. 2890, as amended) and Guidance, Annex 3, Chapter E, paras E.47–E.49).

General considerations are set out for certain types of appropriate person, in particular:

(a)   commercial enterprises;
(b)   trusts;
(c)   charities; and
(d)   social housing landlords;

to take account of the particular circumstances in which such organisations find themselves. Generally, if the social cost of requiring such bodies to pay their full share outweighs the benefit to be obtained by remediation, a lesser amount should be recovered by the authority (Guidance, Annex 3, Chapter D, paras E.20–E.31). This is not to be the case if the organisation has so structured itself deliberately to evade liability.

Other factors to bear in mind include:

(a)   whether the appropriate person is being served with a remediation notice in a private or a business capacity, the latter perhaps being differently treated as he or she will have profited from the operations which caused the problem;

(b)   whether other appropriate persons could or should have been found and thus required to participate in the expense, or the location of them could have enabled this person to escape liability by exclusion or apportionment (Guidance, Annex 3, Chapter E, Pt 5).

As far as owner/occupiers are concerned, the Guidance suggests the following considerations as being relevant:

(a)   whether the owner/occupier took reasonable precautions before purchase, knew of the contamination at purchase and whether the price was reduced accordingly;

(b)   whether the costs are likely to exceed the value of the land, bearing in mind that windfall gains in value to the current owner at public expense should be avoided;

(c)   increases in the land value attributable to the remediation; and

(d)   support from public funds available to develop the land (Guidance, Annex 3, Chapter E, paras E. 38–E.49).

Domestic home-owners should pay only that which they can afford, so long as they can establish that they could not reasonably have known of the contamination at the time of purchase (Guidance, Annex 3, Chapter E, paras E.44–E.46).

Costs may include interest if the appropriate person is both the original polluter and the current owner of the contaminated land (EPA 1990, s. 78P(4)).

The relevant authority also has the power to serve a charging notice on the owner which will constitute a charge on the premises which consist of or include the contaminated land in question. The costs of any charge may be paid by instalments over a maximum 30–year period (EPA 1990, s. 78P(5) and (13)). A person served with the charging notice has a right of appeal which must be made to the county court within 21 days of the receipt of the notice (EPA 1990, s. 78P(8)).

Chapter 5
What Procedures Must be Followed?

SERVICE OF NOTICES

The main operative mechanism of the new regime is the remediation notice, served by the authority. Having identified a contaminated site, an authority must serve such a notice — there is no discretion. However, the relevant authority is under a duty to carry out a formal consultation exercise before the notice is served (EPA 1990, s. 78H(1)). This duty does not apply in cases where it appears to the authority that there is an imminent danger of serious harm or pollution of controlled waters (s. 78H(4)).

The authority is also required to notify the appropriate person(s) on whom a notice would be served, the owner of the land, and any person who appears to be in occupation of the whole or part of the land of its intention to serve the notice, at least three months before the date of service of the notice (EPA 1990, s. 78H(3)).

A notice may be served only after this consultation and notification has taken place, the aim being to encourage the voluntary undertaking of works without the service of a notice.

There are also many circumstances in which the authority is not permitted to serve a notice at all, e.g., where:

(a) the enforcing authority is satisfied that a site is contaminated but no remediation works can be specified to be carried out because they would be unreasonably expensive. In such circumstances it must publish a remediation statement setting out the grounds for taking the view that remediation works cannot be specified;

(b) the authority is satisfied that appropriate steps are being, or will be, taken without the service of a notice. In such circumstances, the person who would have received the notice is required to prepare, within a reasonable period, a remediation statement setting out what works will be carried out, and within what period;

(c) the authority itself would be the recipient;

(d) grounds already exist for the exercise by the authority of its own clean-up powers in respect of the site (EPA 1990, s. 78H(5)).

These exceptions do not apply where there is imminent danger of serious harm or serious pollution of controlled waters.

A further restriction is placed upon the authority in that it cannot issue a notice where powers are available to the Environment Agency in relation to remediation of pollution caused by prescribed processes.

The CL(E)R 2000, regs 4 and 5 specify the content of notices (see also section 3.5), and on whom copies should be served.

Guidance reminds authorities that they should not consider serving a remediation notice at all if they already know that they have no intention of ultimately seeking to recover all, or even some, of the costs from the person served, due to the potential hardship caused (Guidance, Annex 3, Chapter E).

COMPENSATION SCHEMES

A remediation notice can require an appropriate person to carry out works which he or she is otherwise entitled to do, because, for example, he or she is no longer in possession of the site and has no rights of access to it (EPA 1990, s. 78G(1)). In these circumstances, the owner or occupier of land has a statutory obligation to allow remediation works to be carried out on land or waters which he or she owns or occupies (EPA 1990, s. 78G(2)).

Before the remediation notice is served, the enforcing authority has to use its reasonable endeavours to consult with all those parties who might be required to grant rights to the party carrying out the remediation works, though this requirement does not apply where there is imminent danger of serious harm etc. (EPA 1990, s. 78G(3), (4)). No provision is made in the 1990 Act for forcing or expediting the consent of those parties should they refuse. Where rights are granted, compensation will be payable by the appropriate person (EPA 1990, s. 78G(5)). The cost of compensation could, of course, be greater than the cost of carrying out the remediation works themselves.

The CL(E)R 2000, reg. 6 and sch. 2 provide the formula for assessing compensation, and the procedure to be followed. Broadly, this mirrors the regime in the Land Compensation Act 1961.

The statutory guidance provides that the cost of compensating the occupier for rights of access is to be one of the costs to be identified by the authority in, and borne by the appropriate person receiving, the remediation notice (Guidance, Annex 4, paras 21–38).

APPEALS

There is a right of appeal against a remediation notice (EPA 1990, s. 78L(1)). Where the notice is served by a local authority an appeal is heard in the magistrates' court and is to be made by way of summary application. Where the Environment Agency is the appropriate authority the appeal is heard by the Secretary of State.

The time limit for an appeal is 21 days beginning with the first day of service of the remediation notice.

The notice can be quashed if there is a 'material defect' in it. The notice can also be modified or confirmed (EPA 1990, s. 78L(2)).

The CL(E)R 2000, reg. 7 provides numerous grounds of appeal, including:

(a)   the appellant is not the appropriate person;

(b)   someone else is the appropriate person (the appellant must specify who and where they are);

(c)   the authority failed to exclude the appellant from the definition in accordance with guidance;

(d)   the authority improperly apportioned the costs of remediation;

(e)   the authority served a notice when it was statutorily prevented from doing so;

(f)   the notice requires works to be done in respect of controlled waters by an owner or occupier liable in that capacity only;

(g)   the notice requires works to be done in respect of migrated matter on other land;

(h)   the notice requires works to be done in respect of matters governed by other regulatory regimes (e.g., IPPC);

(i)   the land has been improperly identified as contaminated bearing in mind the relevant guidance;

(j)   the authority could not reasonably have taken the view that the land represented an imminent danger of significant harm as defined by guidance;

(k)   the authority has unreasonably refused to accept that voluntary works are being or will be carried out;

(l)   the notice's requirements are unreasonable having regard to the costs and benefits;

(m)   the notice's requirements fail to take account of guidance from the Secretary of State or the Environment Agency (e.g., are insufficiently precise etc.);

(n)   the period of time for compliance is insufficient.

Regulation 14 specifies that an appeal suspends the operation of a remediation notice.

It is tempting to suggest that with so many grounds of appeal, so many technical hurdles to be overcome in the process of designation, identification, exclusion and apportionment, and the benefit of suspension pending the hearing, to appeal a notice will become standard practice in almost every case. It had been the Government's intention to avoid the American experience of litigation over this whole area, but it is clear that it has not been possible to stop falling into similar traps.

REGISTERS

Every enforcing authority must keep a register accessible by the public (EPA 1990, s. 78R(1)). The register will contain details of:

(a)   remediation notices;

(b)   charging notices;

(c) appeals against remediation and charging notices;
(d) remediation statements and declarations;
(e) other environmental controls;
(f) designations of special sites;
(g) notices terminating the designation of special sites;
(h) notifications by owners/occupiers/appropriate persons of any voluntary works which they claim have been carried out on the site; and
(i) convictions for relevant offences;
(j) Agency site-specific guidance.

The fact that information is contained on the register which specifies what voluntary works have allegedly been carried out, is not to be taken as a representation by the authority that the works have in fact been carried out, or how successfully (EPA 1990, s. 78R(3)).

Access can be had to these registers by members of the public, free of charge, and copies provided on the payment of reasonable fees (EPA 1990, s. 78R(8)).

There are certain exclusions from the register for information affecting national security and commercially confidential information (EPA 1990, ss. 78S and 78T).

The CL(E)R 2000, reg. 15 and sch. 3 set out what information is to be provided, and where and how it is to be made available.

The Freedom of Access to Environmental Information Regulations 1992 (SI 1992 No. 3240) provide a public right of access to any information relating to the environment held by public authorities, subject to any exceptions contained in the Regulations themselves, one of which is that the information is incomplete. *Maile* v *Wigan MBC*, May 1999 (unreported), concerning the application of this rule in the context of contaminated land, held that a local authority which was in the process of compiling its data banks regarding possible contamination in its area was not under any obligation to reveal the information it had already compiled, as the work was ongoing and the Regulations awarded access to information only, not half-baked speculation or conjecture. With this in mind, it is likely that applications for such information made under these Regulations will not succeed until the 15-month period for formulating the authority's strategic approach has expired (in July 2001).

Chapter 6
The Implications of the Regime

IMPLICATIONS FOR PROPERTY TRANSACTIONS

In any transaction involving the purchase of property, the general concerns are that:

(a)   a costly environmental liability may be inherited by the buyer, the lender or other professional advisers; or

(b)   the value of the property or site may be adversely affected, even to the point of its being unsaleable, as a consequence of some actual or perceived environmental contamination problem with the site or neighbouring property.

The network of environmental liabilities, particularly regarding contaminated land, is complex, and the price that buyers will pay for sites which they know or believe to be polluted is very volatile. Buyers with experience of foreign jurisdictions may be particularly sensitised to the issue. However, with some relatively cheap and easy steps, an adequate view can be taken of the risks involved in any transaction, which can then be used to inform the decision whether to proceed at all and, if so, with what additional protections.

Liabilities

The environmental liabilities potentially inherited by a buyer of land include the liability for contaminated land discussed in this book, but that is only one of several such risks of which the buyer must be made aware. They may be summarised as follows:

(a)   Criminal liabilities;
(b)   Civil liabilities; and
(c)   Clean-up liabilities.

Criminal liabilities

These include offences under integrated pollution control (IPC) (conducting a prescribed process without or in breach of an authorisation: EPA 1990, s. 23), replaced by pollution prevention and control (PPC) from 31 October 1999 (Pollution Prevention and Control Act 1999, Pollution Prevention and Control (England) Regulations 1999). The offences under the IPC/PPC regimes are related to carrying on 'prescribed processes', such as chemical and metal manufacture. It is an offence to operate such a process without or in breach of a licence to do so. For commercial buyers, it is essential to make an inspection of the public registers if they are taking over the site as a going concern and are intending to carry on the process; but even if not, a run-down of the past track record of the site will assist in assessing the potential risk posed by the site, especially if any accidents or incidents are recorded.

Under s. 33 of the EPA 1990, it is a criminal offence to dispose of controlled waste on a site without or in breach of a licence. This largely, though not exclusively, relates to operative landfill sites. For commercial buyers of land comprising a closed landfill site, it is unlikely that any action would be taken against them in respect of historic events on the site, as there are defences to such prosecutions available for innocent occupiers. It would be a sensible step to make enquiries as to whether a site has been used as a landfill in the past, in order to assess whether any risks are ongoing, as other liabilities may emerge over time from the migration of gases or liquids from the site.

In relation to contaminated land, failure to remediate when instructed to do so is a criminal offence under the EPA 1990, Pt IIA. This may come about as a result of substances already in the land at completion, which are giving rise to a risk of significant harm to persons or things nearby. A buyer of a site can qualify as the 'original polluter'; but even if an original polluter of the land cannot be found, the current owner or occupier may be served with a remediation notice requiring the land to be cleaned up. An offence is committed if he or she fails to comply, and the authorities can carry out the necessary works themselves and recover the costs from the person served with the notice.

Section 79 of the EPA 1990 lists certain statutory nuisances, failure to abate which when required to do so is a criminal offence under s. 80. Statutory nuisances are noises, smells, dust, odour or effluvia which may be a pollution or health risk. Nothing can be a statutory nuisance to the extent that it consists of or comprises land in a contaminated state (Environment Act 1995, sch. 22, para. 89). Buyers of land can be served with abatement notices in respect of any nuisances continuing after the date of purchase, as it may be said that they are the persons responsible for the continuing nuisance. Otherwise they may be liable as owners or occupiers if the person responsible cannot be found.

With regard to the pollution of controlled waters, ss. 85 and 161A of the Water Resources Act 1991 provide for the offences of polluting water without or in breach of a licence, and failing to clean up water when instructed to do so. If a person causes or knowingly permits any polluting matter to enter 'controlled waters' (virtually any watercourse other than a sewer), an offence is committed. Any deliberate or inadvertent leakages of substances from a site which get into watercourses, either directly or via the drainage system, may give rise to a liability. No intention to commit the offence need be shown, only a causal chain of events from the activities of the owner on-site leading to the emission into the waters. Problems afflict buyers with regard to water pollution offences occurring before completion but persisting afterwards, as it may be said that the buyer has knowingly permitted the offence to continue if the buyer ought to have known or realised, or could have found out, that there was a possibility of water pollution occurring from the site.

As far as sewers are concerned, discharging trade effluent to sewer without or in breach of a licence is an offence under s. 118 of the Water Industry Act 1991. This offence relates to ongoing discharges of trade effluent to sewer for an operative site and would really be relevant only when buying a business as a going concern, though it is conceivable that if substances are getting into the sewerage system by migration or leakage, an offence could be committed by the new owner of the site.

Civil liabilities

Civil liabilities include the tort of nuisance (*Cambridge Water Company* v *Eastern Counties Leather plc* [1994] 2 AC 264). (See also *Graham* v *ReChem*, reported in ENDS June 1995, p. 18 and, on the question of land valuation and damages, *Blue Circle Industries plc* v *Ministry of Defence* [1998] 3 All ER 385 (CA) and *English Partnerships* v *Mott Macdonald*, October 1998 (unreported, but see ENDS Report 291, April 1999, p. 25).)

Buyers of land giving rise to a nuisance will be liable for continuing nuisances created by predecessors in title if they knew or ought to have known of the nuisance, could reasonably have foreseen it causing harm, and could have taken reasonable steps to prevent or abate it, but failed to do so. Buyers must therefore take any such reasonable steps to stop ongoing pollution if they are to avoid such liability at some point in the future.

Clean-up liabilities

Clean-up liabilities include those for:

(a)   IPC (EPA 1990, s. 27) or PPC (Pollution Prevention and Control Act 1999, Pollution Prevention and Control (England) Regulations 2000);
(b)   controlled waste (EPA 1990, s. 59);
(c)   contaminated land (EPA 1990, Pt IIA);
(d)   statutory nuisances (EPA 1990, s. 81); and
(e)   water pollution (Water Resources Act 1991, s. 161A).

All these powers apply in circumstances where an offence has been committed, a notice has been served on the owner of the land, and he or she has failed to comply with it. The authorities may enter onto the site and undertake any necessary works, and recover the cost from the person served with the notice.

Other risks

Of equal importance to the buyer of any site is the risk that at some point in the future the property may be rendered unsaleable, or its valuation significantly reduced, if it becomes known that a pollution problem exists, or has existed, on the site. This is largely dictated by the perception of the risk as much as by actuality, and as the perception of environmental risks is often worse than the reality, it is difficult to cater for or quantify. One would, however, expect a prudent commercial buyer of land to expect to negotiate a reduction in price to take account of any environmental risks. Price reductions could have the effect of relieving a seller of liability for contaminated land, leaving only the buyer exposed to the costs of clean-up. Nevertheless, an accurate assessment of price effects should be undertaken as soon as possible, preferably in conjunction with valuers.

The steps to take

Generally

All land is second-hand, so when buying property it is essential to bear in mind — and provide for — the possibility that the buyer will inherit some or all of the liabilities attaching to the site, or suffer a diminution in value in the future. It is not always the polluter who pays but occasionally the current owner, so buyers have to be vigilant. *Caveat emptor* is still all-important.

Often the perception of the environmental risks on a site is worse than the reality, and steps to alleviate or remove the problem may actually be less costly than imagined, and thus a less significant matter. A choice will need to be made by the client as to how much to spend on the investigations, though commercial search organisations and value-added data providers will now provide informative studies quite cheaply, and these should perhaps now be routinely suggested to a buyer.

Other publications address the issues on land transactions more fully than is possible here, so the following comments relate to contaminated land only. Readers are reminded of the existence of other potential liabilities.

Step 1: Advise the client of the potential for problems

It is essential not to overstate the risk that a purchaser client may have to bear the cost of clean-ups, as there is a very long road to travel before that conclusion is reached. However, to ignore it completely is potentially negligent. The possible follow-up steps which could be taken to investigate any likely risk further — and possible cost implications — should be discussed with the client at the initial stage.

Step 2: Make full enquiries of the seller

Solicitors should include specific environmental enquiries in their standard forms of Pre-contract Enquiries. Too many clearly irrelevant enquiries will merely induce the seller to issue a blanket response indicating that the buyer should 'rely on his own enquiries'. Specifically targeted enquiries may elicit a better response.

Amongst other things, enquiries should deal with.

(a)   any contact, discussion, liaison or dispute with the regulatory bodies regarding inspection or designation of the site as contaminated;

(b)   details of any pollution incidents or accidents affecting the site and copies of any reports, correspondence, court orders, notices (including in particular remediation, charging or works notices) or recommendations relating to such accidents or incidents, and details of any remedial work carried out including certificates of satisfactory completion;

(c)   whether the seller is aware of any potentially contaminative current or previous use of the site or neighbouring sites;

(d)   details of previous owners or occupiers and activities carried on by them (to facilitate identification of other polluters should a designation be made that the site is contaminated);

(e)   what (if any) planning consents have been issued in respect of the site, what conditions they contained regarding contamination and its remediation, and details of any works carried out in compliance with them.

Step 3: Make enquiries of the statutory and regulatory bodies

The main bodies to contact are:

(a)   the Environment Agency (for special sites); and
(b)   the local authority;

making full searches of any public registers regarding the site and adjacent land.

Enquiries should be made regarding:

- actual designations made
- notices served or to be served
- works required or undertaken
- formal statements made regarding the land
- appeals
- convictions
- information held by them about the site, any investigations or inspections made of it or adjacent land, details of any accidents, incidents or complaints and an indication of whether there is any intention to investigate further
- accidents, incidents and complaints by regulators or others relating to adjacent land.

Searches from commercial search companies and value-added data providers will usually include details obtainable from the public registers.

Development work is continuing between the Law Society and the Environment Agency on the drafting of a standard form of enquiry for use when making searches of that body. Recent concerns for the Environment Agency surround difficulties in relation to the Data Protection legislation which, in the Environment Agency's view, restricts it from releasing any information which contains personal data relating to a site or its occupants, without the consent of those occupants. This would mean delay and inconvenience if consent were not given.

New enquiries have been added to Form Con 29 as a result of consultations between the Law Society and local authorities, which seek to identify all the information which a local authority is required to compile for the purposes of the official registers which the authority must maintain under the EPA 1990, Pt IIA. However, such information need only appear on the register if land is actually designated as contaminated; and it may be arguable that if land is not so designated, no information need be revealed in answer to the new enquiries. Nevertheless, information regarding the actual state of the land (albeit not yet 'contaminated') may be in the possession of the authority and may be of interest to a purchaser. In such cases, consideration should be given to widening the scope of the enquiry and the wording of the new questions.

Information, in the widest sense, is to be made publicly available under the terms of the Freedom of Access to Environmental Information Regulations 1992 (SI 1992 No. 3240). It is possible to ask regulatory bodies, under these Regulations, whether they hold any information relating to the possible contamination of sites. The Regulations, in force from 31 December 1992, override any other, more restrictive, rights of access.

The 1992 Regulations require that relevant persons holding past or present information relating to the environment make that information available to anyone who requests it, within two months maximum, at a charge no more than is reasonably attributable to the supply of the information. Any grounds for a refusal to provide the information must be given.

'Relevant persons' are public authorities or bodies with public responsibilities for the environment and under the control of public authorities (this may include privatised utility companies).

'Information' means records, registers, reports etc. available in an accessible form (i.e., written, visual, oral or database).

'Relating to the environment' means relating to the state of any water/air, any flora/fauna, any soil, any natural site or other land, or to any 'measures or activities' which may harm, or which may be intended to protect, anything so mentioned.

Step 4: Undertake independent site history investigations

These investigations may include:

(a)   desk-top studies of the site, involving consideration of old maps, plans, photographs and local physical and anecdotal evidence, to evaluate potential risks;

(b)   consideration of contaminated land profiles issued by the DETR, which outline the usual types of contamination associated with certain types of land use (e.g., landfill, railway yards, gasworks, munitions factories etc.);

(c)   obtaining a site investigation report from a commercial search company or value-added data provider, most likely a member of the Environmental Data Association.

The Environmental Data Association's stated mission is to establish and maintain high professional standards in supplying site-specific environmental information to property owners, property buyers and all those professionally involved in advising on property transactions in the United Kingdom. To this end, the Association has adopted a Code of Practice, which its members have agreed to observe. The intention is that commercial searches of this type will be offered in standard form for around £100.

Step 5: Initiate a full site investigation by environmental consultants

This should be commonplace in most commercial cases, as the nature or value of the transaction, and the size of the potential liabilities, would usually justify the cost involved.

Clearly the scope for detailed surveys of potentially contaminated sites is enormous. Clients naturally wish to avoid unnecessary additional costs in relation to their acquisition. Nevertheless, the risks can be great and the costs of the detailed site investigation may well be justified in certain circumstances.

It will generally be in the seller's interests that the buyer knows the full state of the site prior to exchange, so an investigation at joint expense may be negotiable.

It is now increasingly common for indemnities to be sought by a seller — or by the investigating consultant — against any liabilities triggered by the investigation itself, as it is possible for a consultant to become a Class A appropriate person as a result of such activities (see p. 26 above).

Step 6: Consider contractual protections against seller

These may include:

(a)   requiring the seller to make a specifically quantified and earmarked payment or price reduction, to take account of the potential liability;

(b)   requiring the seller to provide full information about the contamination to the buyer in the contract;

(c)   agreeing a formula whereby remediation costs are shared between potential polluters;

(d)   seeking appropriate warranties as to the state of the site at completion;

(e)   seeking an indemnity against future liabilities or reductions in value due to the state of the land at completion;

(f)   requiring remediation by the seller before completion;
(g)   obtaining assignment of any environmental insurance policies which may cover the site (or obtaining fresh cover).

This is a matter for the relative bargaining power of the parties. It is increasingly common for buyers or lessees to insist upon warranties and indemnities in respect of contamination issues. The liabilities that can arise on pollution incidents can be heavy, and therefore the value of such contractual terms may be limited by the financial means of the seller or any guarantor. The individual protections are considered further below.

Specific payments or price reductions   The buyer may seek a reduction in the price (as opposed to a retention, see below) to cover the cost of remediation or clean-up, or any perceived blighting effect on value. Alternatively, the buyer may want the seller to make a payment towards the cost of remediation.

The buyer should be aware that if such payments are made, this may have the effect of removing the seller from the category of persons eligible to receive a remediation notice in respect of contaminated land. If this occurs, the buyer would have to foot the seller's share of any clean-up costs, in addition to any liability of his or her own (Guidance, Annex 3, Chapter D, Pt 5, para. D.43; and see p. 27 above). Buyers may not wish this to occur (though a seller will) and should therefore note the following points.

For a price reduction to be sufficient to count as a 'relevant payment' for remediation so as to exclude the seller from the category of appropriate persons for receipt of a remediation notice, it must be explicitly stated in the contract to be for the purpose of particular remediation in respect of specific contamination. Indeed, it must relate to the specific 'significant pollutant linkage' identified by the regulator, and not to some other problem or issue (Guidance, Annex 3, Chapter D, Pt 5, para. D.53).

Further conditions which must be met for this exclusion to apply are that:

(a)   the payment would have been sufficient at the date it was made to pay for the remediation in question;
(b)   the remediation specified would have been effective to cause the land to cease to be contaminated by the specific significant pollutant linkage in question; and
(c)   the remediation has not been carried out effectively or at all (Guidance, Annex 3, Chapter D, Pt 5, para. D.52).

If, for lack of compliance with these specific requirements, a payment does not have the effect of removing the seller from the relevant category, any payment made would likely be taken into account in any decision on the apportionment of the costs of any clean-up works (see p. 29 above).

Requiring the provision of full information   This may seem to add little to the information-gathering process already undertaken. However, it is a way in which a seller can establish precisely that full information has been given to a buyer in relation to the presence of contaminants on the site, their nature and concentration.

The provision of this information would have the effect of removing the seller from the category of persons eligible to receive a remediation notice in respect of contaminated land, thus leaving the buyer to foot the seller's share of the cost in addition to any he or she would already have to bear (see above). There is thus a clear incentive for a seller to give the information, and a corresponding incentive for the buyer to know exactly the state of the site and take decisions about whether to proceed and, if so, at what price.

The Guidance (in Annex 3, Chapter D, Pt 5, para. D.59(d)) provides that the mere offer of inspection facilities may be sufficient to fix the buyer with all the relevant knowledge necessary to exempt the seller, so the seller may take the view that there is no need to go into print on the point in the contract, other than for the evidential reason mentioned above.

It should be noted that this exclusion allows a seller the exemption only if:

(a)   the sale was on arms' length terms;
(b)   no material misrepresentation was made; and
(c)   the seller retained no interest in the land after completion (Guidance, Annex 3, Chapter D, Pt 5, para. D.58).

Agreements on liabilities   The parties may wish to agree between themselves how they wish to apportion any liability for contamination.

When considering the extent of any indemnities to be given, it is essential to decide who must take the risk not only of all existing contamination, but also of the effect of any future contamination, the effects of any future development of the land (which may release earlier contamination) and the risks of changes in environmental legislation. Standards of clean-up need to be agreed, as do the respective contributions. A sliding scale over 3–5 years may be appropriate, as may threshold and cap arrangements for levels of expenditure.

Any such agreement will be honoured by the authority, and all its decisions regarding liability will be taken with the intention of effecting the agreement (Guidance, Annex 3, Chapter D, Pt 5, para. D.38; and see p. 29 above). However, if the effect of the agreement would be to place an additional burden of expense on a person who would benefit from any relaxation of their responsibility to pay their full share, for example because of the hardship it would cause them, then the authority would, in principle, have to pay that share itself, at public expense. In such circumstances, the authority can ignore the whole agreement and apply the rules in the Guidance instead (see p. 27 above).

Such contracts therefore need to contain mechanisms to ensure that if the authority does not honour and implement the agreement as was intended, the parties will indemnify one another to regulate the position between themselves. It would thus be the parties who would bear the risk of one of them being unable to pay their share, rather than the public purse, and this is also intended as an anti-avoidance measure.

Earlier insurance cover: assignment of the policy? The availability of insurance cover in respect of past polluting events should also be considered and investigated with the seller in preliminary enquiries.

Although the current practice of insurers is to limit or exclude liability for such events, older public liability and third-party liability policies were wide enough to cover them and there may still be residual cover under old policies.

If this is possible or likely, specialist brokers might be called in to carry out an investigation into past insurance policies. If cover is available to the seller under these older policies, the indemnity clause in the contract should be coupled with an assignment of the benefit of this policy.

New insurance New insurance cover may be available to the buyer against the risks of liability resulting from contamination or pollution. This will usually be granted only following an environmental risk assessment by specialist consultants appointed or approved by the insurance companies. It will generally be a requirement that any contamination found be cleaned up and an annual environmental audit of pollution control procedures carried out.

The specialist insurance market is limited, but cover is available, albeit at significant rates of premium.

Retention by buyer Alternatively, the buyer may prefer to complete on the basis of a retention from the price sufficient to cover any likely costs of remediation or clean-up. This will enable the buyer to carry out the remediation works rather than rely upon the seller, and this has advantages in terms of quality control and project management.

Indemnities The seller might be required to indemnify the buyer against the costs of remediation or clean-up, or against any damages, loss or injury resulting from any past contamination or pollution of the soil or any water courses or aquifers.

Caps on the level of indemnity are common, and they are only as good as the credit of the person giving them.

Phased indemnities are becoming more common — an arrangement whereby the seller remains liable for the first year, but the buyer gradually assumes part of the risk as the years go by until after, say, 10 years the buyer is wholly liable.

IMPLICATIONS FOR FUNDERS

The position of banks and other lenders has still not been fully resolved, although the policy statements are clear. They are not specifically excluded, but the position with regard to mortgagees in possession is clarified in that the 1990 Act excludes from the definition of 'owner' a mortgagee not in possession (EPA 1990, s. 78A(9)). This means, however, that financial institutions could still be theoretically liable in two general cases:

(a) as original polluter, the person responsible for 'causing or knowingly permitting' the presence of the contamination, if they are in some degree of control over the day-to-day activities of the borrower (Class A); or

(b) as mortgagee in possession under the 'owner' category (Class B).

Whereas it is clear that it is not the intention of the legislation to make funders liable for clean-up merely because they have lent money to someone (there is a specific exclusion to this effect), there is a residual risk of liability if:

(a) the lender did more than lend, and was perhaps controlling or guiding the day-to-day activities of the borrower, in the guise of a shadow director or by reason of representation on the board;

(b) the exclusion is not operative because there is no one else in the class.

Liability under the owner category (Class B) could be avoided by never going into possession but appointing a licensed insolvency practitioner as a receiver, for whom there is specific exemption from liability.

All this nevertheless means that funders must continue to be vigilant and diligent in the steps taken prior to and during a lending arrangement.

IMPLICATIONS FOR CORPORATE TRANSACTIONS

It is not the purpose of this book to explore fully the process of a corporate takeover or acquisition, but in that context certain matters relating to contaminated land are relevant.

Purchasers of assets or shares in a company may well inherit the liability for contaminated land which goes with the site or property portfolio owned by the target company. Full and rigorous due diligence enquiries should therefore be undertaken to ascertain the past land usage and the identity of any former site owners and occupiers, much as in any property transaction.

It is worth noting that certain exclusionary tests which would remove a seller from the Class A liability group will apply in the specific context of a share sale. Exclusion test 2 (the making of a relevant payment, see p. 27 above) applies in any transaction or series of transactions in which land changes hands, and exclusion test 3 (sales with information) likewise applies in any series of such transactions. Moreover, the Guidance provides that the mere provision of the opportunity to inspect a site will, in any transaction since 1990, be sufficient to attach the buyer with all the knowledge he would have had if a full survey had been conducted (see p. 28 above).

The Guidance also provides that any specific contractual arrangement entered into by the parties relating to the allocation of the costs of clean-up should be honoured by the regulatory bodies. This may require some redrafting of existing warranties and indemnities to ensure that such allocation arrangements fall within the acceptance criteria laid down in the Guidance.

IMPLICATIONS FOR PROFESSIONAL ADVISERS

The professional teams most likely to become involved in the discussion of contaminated land issues are surveyors and solicitors.

There is little risk that the act of advising alone would make a professional adviser liable for the cost of clean-up itself, but it is worth noting that the Guidance at least admits of the theoretical possibility that advisers could be included in Class A as an original polluter, in much the same circumstances as a funder, i.e., if they do more than advise and act in some sort of day-to-day control of the polluting activity, perhaps as shadow directors.

While there is an exclusion available for advisers caught in the class, that exclusion may not be operative if the adviser is the only person in the class in the first place.

Generally, in conducting and determining valuations, surveyors will not be taking actual or potential pollution aspects into account. If a buyer wanted specific assistance on this matter, specific instructions would need to be given to the surveying and valuation team.

A solicitor's failure to advise adequately in appropriate cases on the risks associated with buying land could arguably be classed as negligent. Practitioners should alert the client to the fact that there may be problems associated with a site (whether in the form of liabilities or a decreased valuation) and discuss with the client the steps which can be taken to assess the scale of the problem, and to solve it in the most cost-effective way.

Many professional advisers called in to advise on environmental aspects of a transaction may not be covered for such advice under their professional indemnity policies. This is especially true of the surveying profession, who would need specific instruction (and top-up professional indemnity cover) before they are able to assist in advising on environmental matters.

CONCLUSIONS

Some of the difficult issues for the regulatory bodies have already been comprehensively discussed in the context of other sections of this book. Overall, the key difficulties, and thus the barriers to the efficacy of the whole system, may be summarised as follows:

- technically complex definitions
- imprecision in certain definitions — when is a condition or disease such that harm to human health may be classed as significant?
- formulating an acceptable remediation strategy that is cost-effective
- identifying liable parties
- specific formal requirements for paperwork and registers
- overlapping regulatory regimes
- wide-ranging grounds of appeal
- a subtext which emphasises the need for voluntary works rather than mandatory ones.

All these aspects combine to make one of the most complex pieces of legislation yet to hit the statute book. It is difficult to see how the system will work in practice, if it works at all. It is difficult to see the inducement to comply with a notice when it will be so easy to appeal it and buy time. That leads to the conclusion that this system will go the way of the American Superfund, with more being spent in legal fees than on clean-up.

Maybe the whole scheme will turn out to be a huge bluff — everyone will be so scared of its operation and implications that a moderate amount of clean-up will be achieved on a voluntary basis without the need for a shot ever to be fired in anger. The old saying 'If you want peace, prepare for war' may be as true here as anywhere. Only time will tell.

Appendix 1
Environmental Protection Act 1990

PART IIA
CONTAMINATED LAND

78A. Preliminary

(1)   The following provisions have effect for the interpretation of this Part.

(2)   'Contaminated land' is any land which appears to the local authority in whose area it is situated to be in such a condition, by reason of substances in, on or under the land, that—

(a)   significant harm is being caused or there is a significant possibility of such harm being caused; or

(b)   pollution of controlled waters is being, or is likely to be, caused;

and, in determining whether any land appears to be such land, a local authority shall, subject to subsection (5) below, act in accordance with guidance issued by the Secretary of State in accordance with section 78YA below with respect to the manner in which that determination is to be made.

(3)   A 'special site' is any contaminated land—

(a)   which has been designated as such a site by virtue of section 78C(7) or 78D(6) below; and

(b)   whose designation as such has not been terminated by the appropriate Agency under section 78Q(4) below.

(4)   'Harm' means harm to the health of living organisms or other interference with the ecological systems of which they form part and, in the case of man, includes harm to his property.

(5)   The questions—

(a)   what harm is to be regarded as 'significant',

(b)   whether the possibility of significant harm being caused is 'significant',

(c)   whether pollution of controlled waters is being, or is likely to be caused,

shall be determined in accordance with guidance issued for the purpose by the Secretary of State in accordance with section 78YA below.

(6) Without prejudice to the guidance that may be issued under subsection (5) above, guidance under paragraph (a) of that subsection may make provision for different degrees of importance to be assigned to, or for the disregard of,—

 (a) different descriptions of living organisms or ecological systems;

 (b) different descriptions of places; or

 (c) different descriptions of harm to health or property, or other interference;

and guidance under paragraph (b) of that subsection may make provision for different degrees of possibility to be regarded as 'significant' (or as not being 'significant') in relation to different descriptions of significant harm.

(7) 'Remediation' means—

 (a) the doing of anything for the purpose of assessing the condition of—

  (i) the contaminated land in question;

  (ii) any controlled waters affected by that land; or

  (iii) any land adjoining or adjacent to that land;

 (b) the doing of any works, the carrying out of any operations or the taking of any steps in relation to any such land or waters for the purpose—

  (i) of preventing or minimising, or remedying or mitigating the effects of, any significant harm, or any pollution of controlled waters, by reason of which the contaminated land is such land; or

  (ii) of restoring the land or waters to their former state; or

 (c) the making of subsequent inspections from time to time for the purpose of keeping under review the condition of the land or waters;

and cognate expressions shall be construed accordingly.

(8) Controlled waters are 'affected by' contaminated land if (and only if) it appears to the enforcing authority that the contaminated land in question is, for the purposes of subsection (2) above, in such a condition, by reason of substances in, on or under the land, that pollution of those waters is being, or is likely to be caused.

(9) The following expressions have the meaning respectively assigned to them—

'the appropriate Agency' means—

 (a) in relation to England and Wales, the Environment Agency;

 (b) . . .

'appropriate person' means any person who is an appropriate person, determined in accordance with section 78F below, to bear responsibility for any thing which is to be done by way of remediation in any particular case;

'charging notice' has the meaning given by section 78P(3)(b) below;

'controlled waters'—

 (a) in relation to England and Wales, has the same meaning as in Part III of the Water Resources Act 1991; and

 (b) . . .

. . .

'enforcing authority' means—

 (a) in relation to a special site, the appropriate Agency;

 (b) in relation to contaminated land other than a special site, the local authority in whose area the land is situated;

. . .

'local authority' in relation to England and Wales means—

(a)   any unitary authority;

(b)   any district council, so far as it is not a unitary authority;

(c)   the Common Council of the City of London and, as respects the Temples, the Sub-Treasurer of the Inner Temple and the Under-Treasurer of the Middle Temple respectively;

. . .

'notice' means notice in writing;

'notification' means notification in writing;

'owner', in relation to any land in England and Wales, means a person (other than a mortgagee not in possession) who, whether in his own right or as trustee for any other person, is entitled to receive the rack rent of the land, or, where the land is not let at a rack rent, would be so entitled if it were so let;

. . .

'pollution of controlled waters' means the entry into controlled waters of any poisonous, noxious or polluting matter or any solid waste matter;

'prescribed' means prescribed by regulations;

'regulations' means regulations made by the Secretary of State;

'remediation declaration' has the meaning given by section 78H(6) below;

'remediation notice'' has the meaning given by section 78E(1) below;

'remediation statement' has the meaning given by section 78H(7) below;

'required to be designated as a special site' shall be construed in accordance with section 78C(8) below;

'substance' means any natural or artificial substance, whether in solid or liquid form or in the form of a gas or vapour;

'unitary authority' means—

(a)   the council of a county, so far as it is the council of an area for which there are no district councils;

(b)   the council of any district comprised in an area for which there is no county council;

(c)   the council of a London borough;

(d)   the council of a county borough in Wales;

78B.   Identification of contaminated land

(1)   Every local authority shall cause its area to be inspected from time to time for the purpose—

(a)   of identifying contaminated land; and

(b)   of enabling the authority to decide whether any such land is land which is required to be designated as a special site.

(2)   In performing its functions under subsection (1) above a local authority shall act in accordance with any guidance issued for the purpose by the Secretary of State in accordance with section 78R below.

(3)　If a local authority identifies any contaminated land in its area, it shall give notice of that fact to—

　　(a)　the appropriate Agency;

　　(b)　the owner of the land;

　　(c)　any person who appears to the authority to be in occupation of the whole or any part of the land; and

　　(d)　each person who appears to the authority to be an appropriate person; and any notice given under this subsection shall state by virtue of which of paragraphs (a) to (d) above it is given.

(4)　If, at any time after a local authority has given any person a notice pursuant to subsection (3)(d) above in respect of any land, it appears to the enforcing authority that another person is an appropriate person, the enforcing authority shall give notice to that other person—

　　(a)　of the fact that the local authority has identified the land in question as contaminated land; and

　　(b)　that he appears to the enforcing authority to be an appropriate person.

78C.　Identification and designation of special sites

(1)　If at any time it appears to a local authority that any contaminated land in its area might be land which is required to be designated as a special site, the authority—

　　(a)　shall decide whether or not the land is land which is required to be so designated; and

　　(b)　if the authority decides that the land is land which is required to be so designated, shall give notice of that decision to the relevant persons.

(2)　For the purposes of this section 'the relevant persons' at any time in the case of any land are the persons who at that time fall within paragraphs (a) to (d) below that is to say—

　　(a)　the appropriate Agency;

　　(b)　the owner of the land;

　　(c)　any person who appears to the local authority concerned to be in occupation of the whole or any part of the land; and

　　(d)　each person who appears to that authority to be an appropriate person.

(3)　Before making a decision under paragraph (a) of subsection (1) above in any particular case, a local authority shall request the advice of the appropriate Agency, and in making its decision shall have regard to any advice given by that Agency in response to the request.

(4)　If at any time the appropriate Agency considers that any contaminated land is land which is required to be designated as a special site, that Agency may give notice of that fact to the local authority in whose area the land is situated.

(5)　Where notice under subsection (4) above is given to a local authority, the authority shall decide whether the land in question—

　　(a)　is land which is required to be designated as a special site, or

　　(b)　is not land which is required to be so designated,

and shall give notice of that decision to the relevant persons.

(6)   Where a local authority makes a decision falling within subsection (1)(b) or 5(a) above, the decision shall, subject to section 78D below, take effect on the day after whichever of the following events first occurs, that is to say—

(a)   the expiration of the period of twenty-one days beginning with the day on which the notice required by virtue of subsection (1)(b) or, as the case may be, (5)(a) above is given to the appropriate Agency; or

(b)   if the appropriate Agency gives notification to the local authority in question that it agrees with the decision, the giving of that notification; and where a decision takes effect by virtue of this subsection, the local authority shall give notice of that fact to the relevant persons.

(7)   Where a decision that any land is land which is required to be designated as a special site takes effect in accordance with subsection (6) above, the notice given under subsection (1)(b) or, as the case may be, (5)(a) above shall have effect, as from the time when the decision takes effect, as the designation of that land as such a site.

(8)   For the purposes of this Part, land is required to be designated as a special site if, and only if, it is land of a description prescribed for the purposes of this subsection.

(9)   Regulations under subsection (8) above may make different provision for different cases or circumstances or different areas or localities and may, in particular, describe land by reference to the area or locality in which it is situated.

(10)   Without prejudice to the generality of his power to prescribe any description of land for the purposes of subsection (8) above, the Secretary of State, in deciding whether to prescribe a particlar description of contaminated land for those purposes, may, in particular, have regard to—

(a)   whether land of the description in question appears to him to be land which is likely to be in such a condition, by reason of substances in, on or under the land that—

(i)   serious harm would or might be caused, or

(ii)   serious pollution of controlled waters would be, or would be likely to be, caused; or

(b)   whether the appropriate Agency is likely to have expertise in dealing with the kind of significant harm, or pollution of controlled waters, by reason of which land of the description in question is contaminated land.

78D.   Referral of special site decisions to the Secretary of State

(1)   In any case where—

(a)   a local authority gives notice of a decision to the appropriate Agency pursuant to subsection (1)(b) or (5)(b) of section 78C above, but

(b)   before the expiration of the period of twenty-one days beginning with the day on which that notice is so given, that Agency gives the local authority notice that it disagrees with the decision, together with a statement of its reasons for disagreeing, the authority shall refer the decision to the Secretary of State and shall send to him a statement of its reasons for reaching the decision.

(2)   Where the appropriate Agency gives notice to a local authority under paragraph (b) of subsection (1) above, it shall also send to the Secretary of State a copy of the notice and of the statement given under that paragraph.

(3)   Where a local authority refers a decision to the Secretary of State under subsection (1) above, it shall give notice of that fact to the relevant persons.

(4)   Where a decision of a local authority is referred to the Secretary of State under subsection (1) above, he—

    (a)   may confirm or reverse the decision with respect to the whole or any part of the land to which it relates; and

    (b)   shall give notice of this decision on the referral—

        (i)   to the relevant persons; and

        (ii)   to the local authority.

(5)   Where a decision of a local authority is referred to the Secretary of State under subsection (1) above, the decision shall not take effect until the day after that on which the Secretary of State gives the notice required by subsection (4) above to the persons there mentioned and shall then take effect as confirmed or reversed by him.

(6)   Where a decision which takes effect in accordance with subsection (5) above is to the effect that at least some land is land which is required to be designated as a special site, the notice given under subsection (4)(b) above shall have effect, as from the time when the decision takes effect, as the designation of that land as such a site.

(7)   In this section 'the relevant persons' has the same meaning as in section 78C above.

78E.   Duty of enforcing authority to require remediation of contaminated land etc.

(1)   In any case where—

    (a)   any land has been designated as a special site by virtue of section 78C(7) or 78D(6) above, or

    (b)   a local authority has identified any contaminated land (other than a special site) in its area,

the enforcing authority shall, in accordance with such procedure as may be prescribed and subject to the following provisions of this Part, serve on each person who is an appropriate person a notice (in this Part referred to as a 'remediation notice') specifying what that person is to do by way of remediation and the periods within which he is required to do each of the things so specified.

(2)   Different remediation notices requiring the doing of different things by way of remediation may be served on different persons in consequence of the presence of different substances in, on or under any land or waters.

(3)   Where two or more persons are appropriate persons in relation to any particular thing which is to be done by way of remediation, the remediation notice served on each of them shall state the proportion, determined under section 78F(7) below, of the cost of doing that thing which each of them respectively is liable to bear.

(4)   The only things by way of remediation which the enforcing authority may do, or require to be done, under or by virtue of this Part are things which it considers reasonable, having regard to—

    (a)   the cost which is likely to be involved; and

(b)   the seriousness of the harm, or pollution of controlled waters, in question.

(5)   In determining for any purpose of this Part—

(a)   what is to be done (whether by an appropriate person, the enforcing authority or any other person) by way of remediation in any particular case,

(b)   the standard to which any land is, or waters are, to be remediated pursuant to the notice, or

(c)   what is, or is not, to be regarded as reasonable for the purposes of subsection (4) above,

the enforcing authority shall have regard to any guidance issued for the purpose by the Secretary of State.

(6)   Regulations may make provision for or in connection with—

(a)   the form or content of remediation notices; or

(b)   any steps of a procedural nature which are to be taken in connection with, or in consequence of, the service of a remediation notice.

78F.   Determination of the appropriate person to bear responsibility for remediation

(1)   This section has effect for the purpose of determining who is the appropriate person to bear responsibility for any particular thing which the enforcing authority determines is to be done by way of remediation in any particular case.

(2)   Subject to the following provisions of this section, any person, or any of the persons, who caused or knowingly permitted the substances, or any of the substances, by reason of which the contaminated land in question is such land to be in, on or under that land is an appropriate person.

(3)   A person shall only be an appropriate person by virtue of subsection (2) above in relation to things which are to be done by way of remediation which are to any extent referable to substances which he caused or knowingly permitted to be present in, on or under the contaminated land in question.

(4)   If no person has, after reasonable inquiry, been found who is by virtue of subsection (2) above an appropriate person to bear responsibility for the things which are to be done by way of remediation, the owner or occupier for the time being of the contaminated land in question is an appropriate person.

(5)   If, in consequence of subsection (3) above, there are things which are to be done by way of remediation in relation to which no person has, after reasonable inquiry, been found who is an appropriate person by virtue of subsection (2) above, the owner or occupier for the time being of the contaminated land in question is an appropriate person in relation to those things.

(6)   Where two or more persons would, apart from this subsection, be appropriate persons in relation to any particular thing which is to be done by way of remediation, the enforcing authority shall determine in accordance with guidance issued for the purpose by the Secretary of State whether any, and if so which, of them is to be treated as not being an appropriate person in relation to that thing.

(7)   Where two or more persons are appropriate persons in relation to any particular thing which is to be done by way of remediation, they shall be liable to bear

the cost of doing that thing in proportions determined by the enforcing authority in accordance with guidance issued for the purpose by the Secretary of State.

(8)   Any guidance issued for the purposes of subsection (6) or (7) above shall be issued in accordance with section 78YA below.

(9)   A person who has caused or knowingly permitted any substance ('substance A') to be in, or under any land shall also be taken for the purposes of this section to have caused or knowingly permitted there to be in, on or under that land any substance which is there as a result of a chemical reaction or biological process affecting substance A.

(10)   A thing which is to be done by way of remediation may be regarded for the purposes of this Part as referable to the presence of any substance notwithstanding that the thing in question would not have to be done—

(a)   in consequence only of the presence of that substance in any quantity; or

(b)   in consequence only of the quantity of that substance which any particular person caused or knowingly permitted to be present.

78G.   Grant of, and compensation for, rights of entry etc.

(1)   A remediation notice may require an appropriate person to do things by way of remediation, notwithstanding that he is not entitled to do those things.

(2)   Any person whose consent is required before any thing required by a remediation notice may be done shall grant, or join in granting, such rights in relation to any of the relevant land or waters as will enable the appropriate person to comply with any requirements imposed by the remediation notice.

(3)   Before serving a remediation notice, the enforcing authority shall reasonably endeavour to consult every person who appears to the authority—

(a)   to be the owner or occupier of any of the relevant land or waters, and

(b)   to be a person who might be required by subsection (2) above to grant, or join in granting, any rights,

concerning the rights which that person may be so required to grant.

(4)   Subsection (3) above shall not preclude the service of a remediation notice in any case where it appears to the enforcing authority that the contaminated land in question is in such a condition, by reason of substances in, on or under the land, that there is imminent danger of serious harm or serious pollution of controlled waters, being caused.

(5)   A person who grants, or joins in granting, any rights pursuant to subsection (2) above shall be entitled, on making an application within such period as may be prescribed and in such manner as may be prescribed to such person as may be prescribed, to be paid by the appropriate person compensation of such amount as may be determined in such manner as may be prescribed.

(6)   Without prejudice to the generality of the regulations that may be made by virtue of subsection (5) above regulations by virtue of that subsection may make such provision in relation to compensation under this section as may be made by regulations by virtue of subsection (4) of section 35A above in relation to compensation under that section.

(7)   In this section, 'relevant land or waters' means—
  (a)   the contaminated land in question;
  (b)   any controlled waters affected by that land; or
  (c)   any land adjoining or adjacent to that land or those waters.

78H.   Restrictions and prohibitions on serving remediation notices

(1)   Before serving a remediation notice, the enforcing authority shall reasonably endeavour to consult—
  (a)   the person on whom the notice is to be served,
  (b)   the owner of any land to which the notice relates,
  (c)   any person who appears to that authority to be in occupation of the whole or any part of the land, and
  (d)   any person of such other description as may be prescribed,
concerning what is to be done by way of remediation.

(2)   Regulations may make provision for, or in connection with, steps to be taken for the purposes of subsection (1) above.

(3)   No remediation notice shall be served on any person by reference to any contaminated land during any of the following periods, that is to say—
  (a)   the period—
    (i)   beginning with the identification of the contaminated land in question pursuant to section 78B(1) above, and
    (ii)   ending with the expiration of the period of three months beginning with the day on which the notice required by subsection (3)(d) or, as the case may be, (4) of section 78B above is given that person in respect of that land;
  (b)   if a decision falling within paragraph (b) of section 78C(1) above is made in relation to the contaminated land in question, the period beginning with the making of the decision and ending with the expiration of the perod of three months beginning with—
    (i)   in a case where the decision is not referred to the Secretary of State under section 78D above, the day on which the notice required by section 78C(6) above is given, or
    (ii)   in a case where the decision is referred to the Secretary of State under section 78D above, the day on which he gives the notice required by subsection (4)(b) of that section;
  (c)   if the appropriate Agency gives a notice under subsection (4) of section 78C above to a local authority in relation to the contaminated land in question, the period beginning with the day on which that notice is given and endng with the expiration of the period of three months beginning with—
    (i)   in a case where notice is given under subsection (6) of that section, the day on which that notice is given;
    (ii)   in a case where the authority makes a decision falling within subsection (5)(b) of that section and the appropriate Agency fails to give notice under paragraph (b) of section 78D(1) above, the day following the expiration of the period of twenty-one days mentioned in that paragraph; or

(iii)   in a case where the authority makes a decision falling within section 78C(5)(b) above which is referred to the Secretary of State under section 78D above, the day on which the Secretary of State gives the notice required by subsection (4)(b) of that section.

(4)   Neither subsection (1) nor subsection (3) above shall preclude the service of a remediation notice in any case where it appears to the enforcing authority that th land in question is in such a condition, by reason of substances in, on or under the land, that there is imminent danger of serious harm, or serious pollution of controlled waters, being caused.

(5)   The enforcing authority shall not serve a remediation notice on a person if and so long as any one or more of the following conditions is for the time being satisfied in the particular case, that is to say—

(a)   the authority is satisfied, in consequence of section 78E(4) and (5) above, that there is nothing by way of remediation which could be specified in a remediation notice served on that person;

(b)   the authority is satisfied that appropriate things are being, or will be, done by way of remediation without the service of a remediation notice on that person;

(c)   it appears to the authority that the person on whom the notice would be served is the authority itself; or

(d)   the authority is satisfied that the powers conferred on it by section 78N below to do what is appropriate by way of remediation are exercisable.

(6)   Where the enforcing authority is precluded by virtue of section 78E(4) or (5) above from specifying in a remediation notice any particular thing by way of remediation which it would othewise have specified in such a notice, the authority shall prepare and publish a document (in this Part referred to as a 'remediation declaration') which shall record—

(a)   the reasons why the authority would have specified that thing; and

(b)   the grounds on which the authority is satisfied that it is precluded from specifying that thing in such a notice.

(7)   In any case where the enforcing authority is precluded, by virtue of paragraph (b), (c) or (d) of subsection (5) above, from serving a remediation notice, the responsible person shall prepare and publish a document (in this Part referred to as a 'remediation statement') which shall record—

(a)   the things which are being, have been, or are expected to be, done by way of remediation in the particular case;

(b)   the name and address of the person who is doing, has done, or is expected to do, each of those things; and

(c)   the periods within which each of those things is being, or is expected to be, done.

(8)   For the purposes of subsection (7) above, the 'responsible person' is—

(a)   in a case where the condition in paragraph (b) of subsection (5) above is satisfied, the person who is doing or has done, or who the enforcing authority is satisfied will do, the things there mentioned; or

(b)   in a case where the condition in paragraph (c) or (d) of that subsection is satisfied, the enforcing authority.

(9)   If a person who is required by virtue of subsection (8)(a) above to prepare and publish a remediation statement fails to do so within a reasonable time after the date on which a remediation notice specifying the things there mentioned could, apart from subsection (5) above, have been served, the enforcing authority may itself prepare and publish the statement and may recover its reasonable costs of doing so from that person.

(10)   Where the enforcing authority has been precluded by virtue only of subsection (5) above from serving a remediation notice on an appropriate person but—

(a)   none of the conditions in that subsection is for the time being satisified in the particular case, and

(b)   the authority is not precluded by any other provison of this Part from serving a remediation notice on that appropriate person,

the authority shall serve a remediation notice on that person; and any such notice may be so served without any further endeavours by the authority to consult persons pursuant to subsection (1) above, if and to the extent that that person has been consulted pursuant to that subsection concerning the things which will be specified in the notice.

78J.   Restrictions on liability relating to the pollution of controlled waters

(1)   This section applies where any land is contaminated land by virtue of paragraph (b) of subsection (2) of section 78A above (whether or not the land is also contaminated land by virtue of paragraph (a) of that subsection).

(2)   Where this section applies, no remediation notice given in consequence of the land in question being contaminated land shall require a person who is an appropriate person by virtue of section 78F(4) or (5) above to do anything by way of remediation to that or any other land, or any waters, which he could not have been required to do by such a notice had paragraph (b) of section 78A(2) above (and all other references to pollution of controlled waters) been omitted from this Part.

(3)   If, in a case where this section applies, a person permits, has permitted, or might permit, water from an abandoned mine or part of a mine—

(a)   to enter any controlled waters, or

(b)   to reach a place from which it is or, as the case may be, was likely, in the opinion of the enforcing authority, to enter such waters,

no remediation notice shall require him in consequence to do anything by way of remediation (whether to the contaminated land in question or to any other land or waters) which he could not have been required to do by such a notice had paragraph (b) of section 78A(2) above (and all other references to pollution of controlled waters) been omitted from this Part.

(4)   Subsection (3) above shall not apply to the owner or former operator of any mine or part of a mine if the mine or part in question became abandoned after 31st December 1999.

(5)   In determining for the purposes of subsection (4) above whether a mine or part of a mine became abandoned before, on or after 31st December 1999 in a case where the mine or part has become abandoned on two or more occasions, of which—

(a)   at least one falls on or before that date, and

(b)   at least one falls after that date,

the mine or part shall be regarded as becoming abandoned after that date (but without prejudice to the operation of subsection (3) above in relation to that mine or part at, or in relation to, any time before the first of those occasions which fall after that date).

(6)   Where, immediately before a part of a mine becomes abandoned, that part is the only part of the mine not falling to be regarded as abandoned for the time being, the abandonment of that part shall not be regarded for the purposes of subsection (4) or (5) above as constituting the abandonment of the mine, but only of that part of it.

(7)   Nothing in subsection (2) or (3) above prevents the enforcing authority from doing anything by way of remediation under section 78N below which it could have done apart from that subsection, but the authority shall not be entitled under section 78P below to recover from any person any part of the cost incurred by the authority in doing by way of remediation anything which it is precluded by subsection (2) or (3) above from requiring that person to do.

(8)   In this section 'mine' has the same meaning as in the Mines and Quarries Act 1954.

78K.   Liability in respect of contaminating substances which escape to other land

(1)   A person who has caused or knowingly permitted any substances to be in, on or under any land shall also be taken for the purposes of this Part to have caused or, as the case may be, knowingly permitted those substances to be in, on or under any other land to which they appear to have escaped.

(2)   Subsections (3) and(4) below apply in any case where it appears that any substances are or have been in, on or under any land (in this section referred to as 'land A') as a result of their escape, whether directly or indirectly from other land in, on or under which a person caused or knowingly permitted them to be.

(3)   Where this subsection applies, no remediation notice shall require a person—

(a)   who is the owner or occupier of land A, and

(b)   who has not caused or knowingly permitted the substances in question to be in, on or under that land,

to do anything by way of remediation to any land or waters (other than land or waters of which he is the owner or occupier) in consequence of land A appearing to be in such a condition, by reason of the presence of those substances in, on or under it, that significant harm is being caused, or there is a significant possibility of such harm being caused, or that pollution of controlled waters is being, or is likely to be caused.

(4)   Where this subsection applies, no remediation notice shall require a person—

(a)   who is the owner or occupier of land A, and

(b)   who has not caused or knowingly permitted the substances in question to be in, on or under that land, to do anything by way of remediation in consequence of any further land in, on or under which those substances or any of them appear to be or to have been present as a result of their escape from land A ('land B') appearing to be in such a condition, by reason of the presence of those substances in, on or under it, that significant harm is being caused, or there is a significant possibility of such harm being caused, or that pollution of controlled waters is being, or is likely to be caused, unless he is also the owner or occupier of land B.

(5)   In any case where—

(a)   a person ('person A') has caused or knowingly permitted any substances to be in, on, or under any land,

(b)   another person ('person B') who has not caused or knowingly permitted those substances to be in, or under that land becomes the owner or occupier of that land, and

(c)   the substances, or any of the substances, mentioned in paragraph (a) above appear to have escaped to other land,

no remediation notice shall require person B to do anything by way of remediation to that other land in consequence of the apparent acts or omissions of person A, except to the extent that person B caused or knowingly permitted the escape.

(6)   Nothing in subsection (3), (4) or (5) above prevents the enforcing authority from doing anything by way of remediation under section 78N below which it could have done apart from that subsection, but the authority shall not be entitled under section 78P below to recover from any person any part of the cost incurred by the authority in doing by way of remediation anything which it is precluded by subsection (3), (4) or (5) above from requiring that person to do.

(7)   In this section, 'appear' means appear to the enforcing authority, and cognate expressions shall be construed accordingly.

78L.   Appeals against remediation notices

(1)   A person on whom a remediation notice is served may, within the period of twenty-one days beginning with the day on which the notice is served, appeal against the notice—

(a)   if it was served by a local authority, to a magistrates' court or, . . . or

(b)   if it was served by the appropriate Agency, to the Secretary of State;

and in the following provisions of this section 'the appellate authority' means the magistrates' court, the sheriff or the Secretary of State, as the case may be.

(2)   On any appeal under subsection (1) above the appellate authority—

(a)   shall quash the notice, if it is satisfied that there is a material defect in the notice; but

(b)   subject to that, may confirm the remediation notice, with or without modification, or quash it.

(3)   Where an appellate authority confirms a remediation notice, with or without modification, it may extend the period specified in the notice for doing what the notice requires to be done.

(4)   Regulations may make provision with respect to—

(a)   the grounds on which appeals under subsection (1) above may be made;

(b)   the cases in which, grounds on which, court or tribunal to which, or person at whose instance, an appeal against a decision of a magistrates' court or sheriff court in pursuance of an appeal under subsection (1) above shall lie; or

(c)   the procedure on an appeal under subsection (1) above or on an appeal by virtue of paragraph (b) above.

(5)   Regulations under subsection (4) above may (among other things)—

(a)   include provisions comparable to those in section 290 of the Public Healh Act 1936 (appeals against notices requiring the execution of works);

(b)   prescribe the cases in which a remediation notice is, or is not, to be suspended until the appeal is decided, or until some other stage in proceedings;

(c)   prescribe the cases in which the decision on an appeal may in some respects be less favourable to the appellant than the remediation notice against which he is appealing;

(d)   prescribe the cases in which the appellant may claim that a remediation notice should have been served on some other person and prescribe the procedure to be followed in those cases;

(e)   make provision as respects—

(i)   the particulars to be included in the notice of appeal;

(ii)   the persons on whom notice of appeal is to be served and the particulars, if any, which are to accompany the notice; and

(iii)   the abandonment of an appeal;

(f)   make different provision for different cases or classes of case.

(6)   This section, so far as relating to appeals to the Secretary of State, is subject to section 114 of the Environment Act 1995 (delegation or reference of appeals etc).

78M.   Offences of not complying with a remediation notice

(1)   If a person on whom an enforcing authority serves a remediation notice fails, without reasonable excuse, to comply with any of the requirements of the notice, he shall be guilty of an offence.

(2)   Where the remediation notice in question is one which was required by section 78E(3) above to state, in relation to the requirement which has not been complied with, the proportion of the cost involved which the person charged with the offence is liable to bear, it shall be a defence for that person to prove that the only reason why he has not complied with the requirement is that one or more of the other persons who are liable to bear a proportion of that cost refused, or was not able, to comply with the requirement.

(3)   Except in a case falling within subsection (4) below, a person who commits an offence under subsection (1) above shall be liable, on summary conviction, to a fine not exceeding level 5 on the standard scale and to a further fine of an amount equal to one-tenth of level 5 on the standard scale for each day on which the failure continues after conviction of the offence and before the enforcing authority has begun to exercise its powers by virtue of section 78N(3)(c) below.

(4)   A person who commits an offence under subsection (1) above in a case where the contaminated land to which the remediation notice relates is industrial, trade or business premises shall be liable on summary conviction to a fine not exceeding £20,000 or such greater sum as the Secretary of State may from time to time by order substitute and to a further fine of an amount equal to one-tenth of that sum for each day on which the failure continues after conviction of the offence and before the enforcing authority has begun to exercise its powers by virtue of section 78N(3)(c) below.

(5)   If the enforcing authority is of the opinion that proceedings for an offence under this section would afford an ineffectual remedy against a person who has failed to comply with any of the requirements of a remediation notice which that authority has served on him, that authority may take proceedings in the High Court . . . for the purpose of securing compliance with the remediation notice.

(6)   In this section 'industrial, trade or business premises' means premises used for any industrial, trade or business purposes or premises not so used on which matter is burnt in connection with any industrial, trade or business process, and premises are used for industrial purposes where they are used for the purposes of any treatment or process as well as where they are used for the purpose of manufacturing.

(7)   No order shall be made under subsection (4) above unless a draft of the order has been laid before, and approved by a resolution of, each House of Parliament.

78N.   Powers of the enforcing authority to carry out remediation

(1)   Where this section applies, the enforcing authority shall itself have power, in a case falling within paragraph (a) or (b) of section 78E(1) above, to do what is appropriate by way of remediation to the relevant land or waters.

(2)   Subsection (1) above shall not confer power on the enforcing authority to do anything by way of remediation if the authority would, in the particular case, be precluded by section 78YB below from serving a remediation notice requiring that thing to be done.

(3)   This section applies in each of the following cases, that is to say—

(a)   where the enforcing authority considers it necessary to do anything itself by way of remediation for the purpose of preventing the occurrence of any serious harm, or serious pollution of controlled waters, of which there is imminent danger;

(b)   where an appropriate person has entered into a written agreement with the enforcing authority for that authority to do, at the cost of that person, that which he would otherwise be required to do under this Part by way of remediation;

(c)   where a person on whom the enforcing authority serves a remediation notice fails to comply with any of the requirements of the notice;

(d)   where the enforcing authority is precluded by section 78J or 78K above from including something by way of remediation in a remediation notice;

(e)   where the enforcing authority considers that, were it to do some particular thing by way of remediation, it would decide, by virtue of subsection (2) of section 78P below or any guidance issued under that subsection,—

(i)　not to seek to recover under subsection (1) of that section any of the reasonable cost incurred by it in doing that thing; or

(ii)　to seek so to recover only a portion of that cost;

(f)　where no person has, after reasonable inquiry, been found who is an appropriate person in relation to any particular thing.

(4)　Subject to section 78E(4) and (5) above, for the purposes of this section, the things which it is appropriate for the enforcing authority to do by way of remediation are—

(a)　in a case falling within paragraph (a) of subsection (3) above, anything by way of remediation which the enforcing authority considers necessary for the purpose mentioned in that paragraph;

(b)　in a case falling within paragraph (b) of that subsection, anything specified in, or determined under, the agreement mentioned in that paragraph;

(c)　in a case falling within paragraph (c) of that subsection, anything which the person mentioned in that paragraph was required to do by virtue of the remediation notice;

(d)　in a case falling within paragraph (d) of that subsection, anything by way of remediation which the enforcing authority is precluded by section 78J or 78K above from including in a remediation notice;

(e)　in a case falling within paragraph (e) or (f) of that subsection, the particular thing mentioned in the paragraph in question.

(5)　In this section 'the relevant land or waters' means—

(a)　the contaminated land in question;

(b)　any controlled waters affected by that land; or

(c)　any land adjoining or adjacent to that land or those waters.

78P.　Recovery of, and security for, the cost of remediation by the enforcing authority

(1)　Where, by virtue of section 78N(3)(a), (c), (e) or (f) above, the enforcing authority does any particular thing by way of remediation, it shall be entitled, subject to section 78J(7) and 78K(6) above, to recover the reasonable cost incurred in doing it from the appropriate person or, if there are two or more appropriate persons in proportions determined pursuant to section 78F(7) above.

(2)　In deciding whether to recover the cost, and, if so, how much of the cost, which it is entitled to recover under subsection (1) above, the enforcing authority shall have regard—

(a)　to any hardship which the recovery may cause to the person from whom the cost is recoverable; and

(b)　to any guidance issued by the Secretary of State for the purposes of this subsection.

(3)　Subsection (4) below shall apply in any case where—

(a)　any cost is recoverable under subsection (1) above from a person—

(i)　who is the owner of any premises which consist of or include the contaminated land in question; and

(ii)   who caused or knowingly permitted the substances, or any of the substances, by reason of which the land is contaminated land to be in, on or under the land; and

(b)   the enforcing authority serves a notice under this subsection (in this Part referred to as a 'charging notice') on that person.

(4)   Where this subsection applies—

(a)   the cost shall carry interest, at such reasonable rate as the enforcing authority may determine, from the date of service of the notice until the whole amount is paid; and

(b)   subject to the following provisions of this section, the cost and accrued interest shall be a charge on the premises mentioned in subsection (3)(a)(i) above.

(5)   A charging notice shall—

(a)   specify the amount of the cost which the enforcing authority claims is irrecoverable;

(b)   state the effect of subsection (4) above and the rate of interest determined by the authority under that subsection; and

(c)   state the effect of subsections (7) and (8) below.

(6)   On the date on which an enforcing authority serves a charging notice on a person, the authority shall also serve a copy of the notice on every other person who, to the knowledge of the authority, has an interest in the premises capable of being affected by the charge.

(7)   Subject to any order under subsection (9)(b) or (c) below, the amount of any cost specified in a charging notice and the accrued interest shall be a charge on the premises—

(a)   as from the end of the period of twenty-one days beginning with the service of the charging notice, or

(b)   where an appeal is brought under subsection (8) below, as from the final determination or (as the case may be) the withdrawal, of the appeal,

until the cost and interest are recovered.

(8)   A person served with a charging notice or a copy of a charging notice may appeal against the notice to a county court within the period of twenty-one days beginning with the date of service.

(9)   On an appeal under subsection (8) above, the court may—

(a)   confirm the notice without modification;

(b)   order that the notice is to have effect with the substitution of a different amount for the amount originally specified in it; or

(c)   order that the notice is to be of no effect.

(10)   Regulations may make provision with respect to—

(a)   the grounds on which appeals uner this section may be made; or

(b)   the procedure on any such appeal.

(11)   An enforcing authority shall, for the purpose of enforcing a charge under this section, have all the same powers and remedies under the Law of Property Act 1925, and otherwise, as if it were a mortgagee by deed having powers of sale and lease, of accepting surrenders of leases and of appointing a receiver.

(12)   Where any cost is a charge on premises under this section, the enforcing authority may by order declare the cost to be payable with interest by instalments within the specified period until the whole amount is paid.

(13)   In subsection (12) above—

'interest' means interest at the rate determined by the enforcing authority under subsection (4) above; and

    'the specified period' means such period of thirty years or less from the date of service of the charging notice as is specified in the order.

(14)   . . .

78Q.   Special sites

(1)   If, in a case where a local authority has served a remediation notice, the contaminated land in question becomes a special site, the appropriate Agency may adopt the remediation notice and, if it does so,—

    (a)   it shall give notice of its decision to adopt the remediation notice to the appropriate person and to the local authority;

    (b)   the remediation notice shall have effect, as from the time at which the appropriate Agency decides to adopt it, as a remediation notice given by that Agency; and

    (c)   the validity of the remediation notice shall not be affected by—

       (i)   the contaminated land having become a special site;

       (ii)   the adoption of the remediation notice by the appropriate Agency; or

       (iii)   anything in paragraph (b) above.

(2)   Where a local authority has, by virtue of section 78N above, begun to do anything, or any series of things, by way of remediation—

    (a)   the authority may continue doing that thing, or that series of things, by virtue of that section, notwithstanding that the contaminated land in question becomes a special site; and

    (b)   section 78P above shall apply in relation to the reasonable cost incurred by the authority in doing that thing or those things as if that authority were the enforcing authority.

(3)   If and so long as any land is a special site, the appropriate Agency may from time to time inspect that land for the purpose of keeping its condition under review.

(4)   If it appears to the appropriate Agency that a special site is no longer land which is required to be designated as such a site, the appropriate Agency may give notice—

    (a)   to the Secretary of State, and

    (b)   to the local authority in whose area the site is situated,

terminating the designation of the land in question as a special site as from such date as may be specified in the notice.

(5)   A notice under subsection (4) above shall not prevent the land, or any of the land, to which the notice relates beng designated as a special site on a subsequent occasion.

(6)   In exercising its functions under subsection (3) or (4) above, the appropriate Agency shall act in accordance with any guidance given for the purpose by the Secretary of State.

78R. Registers

(1)   Every enforcing authority shall maintain a register containing prescribed particulars of or relating to—

(a)   remediation notices served by that authority;

(b)   appeals against any such remediation notices;

(c)   remediation statements or remediation declarations prepared and published under section 78H above;

(d)   in relation to an enforcing authority in England and Wales, appeals against charging notices served by that authority;

(e)   notices under subsection (1)(b) or (5)(a) of section 78C above which have effect by virtue of subsection (7) of that section as the designation of any land as a special site;

(f)   notices under subsection (4)(b) of section 78D above which have effect by virtue of subsection (6) of that section as the designation of any land as a special site;

(g)   notices given by or to the enforcing authority under section 78Q(4) above terminating the designation of any land as a special site;

(h)   notifications given to that authority by persons—

(i)   on whom a remediation notice has been served, or

(ii)   who are or were required by virtue of section 78H(8)(a) above to prepare and publish a remediation statement,

of what they claim has been done by them by way of remediation;

(j)   notifications given to that authority by owners or occupiers of land—

(i)   in respect of which a remediation notice has been served, or

(ii)   in respect of which a remediation statement has been prepared and published,

of what they claim has been done on the land in question by way of remediation;

(k)   convictions for such offences under section 78M above as may be prescribed;

(l)   such other matters relating to contaminated land as may be prescribed;

but that duty is subject to sections 78S and 78T below.

(2)   The form of, and the descriptions of information to be contained in, notifications for the purposes of subsection (1)(h) or (j) above may be prescribed by the Secretary of State.

(3)   No entry made in a register by virtue of subsection (1)(h) or (j) above constitutes a repesentation by the body maintaining the register or, in a case where the entry is made by virtue of subsection (6) below, the authority which sent the copy of the particulars in question pursuant to subsection (4) or (5) below—

(a)   that what is stated in the entry to have been done has in fact been done; or

(b)   as to the manner in which it has been done.

(4)   Where any particulars are entered on a register maintained under this section by the appropriate Agency, the appropriate Agency shall send a copy of those

particulars to the local authority in whose area is situated the land to which the particulars relate.

(5) In any case where—

(a) any land is treated by virtue of section 78X(2) below as situated in the area of a local authority other than the local authority in whose area it is in fact situated, and

(b) any particulars relating to that land are entered on the register maintained under this section by the local authority in whose area the land is so treated as situated, that authority shall send a copy of those particulars to the local authority in whose area the land is in fact situated.

(6) Where a local authority receives a copy of any particulars sent to it pursuant to subsection (4) or (5) above, it shall enter those particulars on the register maintained by it under this section.

(7) Where information of any description is excluded by virtue of section 78T below from any register maintained under this section, a statement shall be entered in the register indicating the existence of information of that description.

(8) It shall be the duty of each enforcing authority—

(a) to secure that the registers maintained by it under this section are available, at all reasonable times, for inspection by the public free of charge; and

(b) to afford to members of the public facilities for obtaining copies of entries, on payment of reasonable charges;

and, for the purposes of this subsection, places may be prescribed by the Secretary of State at which any such registers or facilities as are mentioned in paragraph (a) or (b) above are to be available or afforded to the public in pursuance of the paragraph in question.

(9) Registers under this section may be kept in any form.

78S. Exclusion from registers of information affecting national security

(1) No information shall be included in a register maintained under section 78R above if and so long as, in the opinion of the Secretary of State, the inclusion in the register of that information, or information of that description, would be contrary to the interests of national security.

(2) The Secretary of State may, for the purpose of securing the exclusion from registers of information to which subsection (1) above applies, give to enforcing authorities directions—

(a) specifying information, or descriptions of information, to be excluded from their registers; or

(b) specifying descriptions of information to be referred to the Secretary of State for his determination;

and no information referred to the Secretary of State in pursuance of paragraph (b) above shall be in any such register until the Secretary of State determines that it should be so included.

(3) The enforcing authority shall notify the Secretary of State of any information which it excludes from the register in pursuance of directions under subsection (2) above.

(4)   A person may, as respects any information which appears to him to be information to which subsection (1) above may apply, give a notice to the Secretary of State specifying the information and indicating its apparent nature; and, if he does so—

(a)   he shall notify the enforcing authority that he has done so; and

(b)   no information so notified to the Secretary of State shall be included in any such register until the Secretary of State has determined that it should be so included.

78T.   Exclusion from registers of certain confidential information

(1)   No information relating to the affairs of any individual or business shall be included in a register maintained under section 78R above, without the consent of that individual or the person for the time being carrying on that business, if and so long as the information—

(a)   is, in relation to him, commercially confidential; and

(b)   is not required to be included in the register in pursuance of directions under subsection (7) below;

but information is not commercially confidential for the purposes of this section unless it is determined under this section to be so by the enforcing authority or, on appeal, by the Secretary of State.

(2)   Where it appears to an enforcing authority that any information which has been obtained by the authority under or by virtue of any provision of this Part might be commercially confidential, the authority shall—

(a)   give to the person to whom or whose business it relates notice that that information is required to be included in the register unless excluded under this section; and

(b)   give him a reasonable opportunity—

(i)   of objecting to the inclusion of the information on the ground that it is commercially confidential; and

(ii)   of making representations to the authority for the purpose of justifying any such objection;

and, if any representations are made, the enforcing authority shall, having taken the representations into account, determine whether the information is or is not commercially confidential.

(3)   Where, under subsection (2) above, an authority determines that information is not commercially confidential—

(a)   the information shall not be entered in the register until the end of the period of twenty-one days beginning with the date on which the determination is notified to the person concerned;

(b)   that person may appeal to the Secretary of State against the decision;

and, where an appeal is brought in respect of any information, the information shall not be entered in the register until the end of the period of seven days following the day on which the appeal is finally determined or withdrawn.

(4)   An appeal under subsection (3) above shall, if either party to the appeal so requests or the Secretary of State so decides, take or continue in the form of a hearing (which must be held in private).

(5)   Subsection (10) of section 15 above shall apply in relation to an appeal under subsection (3) above as it applies in relation to an appeal under that section.

(6)   Subsection (3) above is subject to section 114 of the Environment Act 1995 (delegation or reference of appeals etc).

(7)   The Secretary of State may give to the enforcing authorities directions as to specified information, or descriptions of information, which the public interest requires to be included in registers maintained under section 78R above notwithstanding that the information may be commercially confidential.

(8)   Information excluded from a register shall be treated as ceasing to be commercially confidential for the purposes of this section at the expiry of the period of four years beginning with the date of the determination by virtue of which it was excluded; but the person who furnished it may apply to the authority for the information to remain excluded from the register on the ground that it is still commercially confidential and the authority shall determine whether or not that is the case.

(9)   Subsections (3) to (6) above shall apply in relation to a determination under subsection (8) above as they apply in relation to a determination under subsection (2) above.

(10)   Information is, for the purposes of any determination under this section, commercially confidential, in relation to any individual or person, if its being contained in the register would prejudice to an unreasonable degree the commercial interests of that individual or person.

(11)   For the purposes of subsection (10) above, there shall be disregarded any prejudice to the commercial interests of any individual or person so far as relating only to the value of the contaminated land in question or otherwise to the ownership or occupation of that land.

78U.   Reports by the appropriate Agency on the state of contaminated land
   (1)   The appropriate Agency shall—
      (a)   from time to time, or
      (b)   if the Secretary of State at any time so requests,
prepare and publish a report on the state of contaminated land in England and Wales . . . as the case may be.

(2)   A local authority shall, at the written request of the appropriate Agency, furnish the appropriate Agency with such information to which this subsection applies as the appropriate Agency may require for the purpose of enabling it to perform its functions under subsection (1) above.

(3)   The information to which subsection (2) above applies is such information as the local authority may have, or may reasonably be expected to obtain, with respect to the condition of contaminated land in its area, being information which the authority has acquired or may acquire in the exercise of its functions under this Part.

78V.   Site-specific guidance by the appropriate Agency concerning contaminated land
   (1)   The appropriate Agency may issue guidance to any local authority with respect to the exercise or performance of the authority's powers or duties under this

Part in relation to any particular contaminated land; and in exercising or performing those powers or duties in relation to that land the authority shall have regard to any such guidance so issued.

(2)   If and to the extent that any guidance issued under subsection (1) above to a local authority is inconsistent with any guidance issued under this Part by the Secretary of State, the local authority shall disregard the guidance under that subsection.

(3)   A local authority shall, at the written request of the appropriate Agency, furnish the appropriate Agency with such information to which this subsection applies as the approprate Agency may require for the purpose of enabling it to issue guidance for the purposes of subsection (1) above.

(4)   The information to which subsection (3) above applies is such information as the local authority may have, or may reasonably be expected to obtain, with respect to any contaminated land in its area, being information which the authority has acquired, or may acquire, in the exercise of its functions under this Part.

78W.   The appropriate Agency to have regard to guidance given by the Secretary of State

(1)   The Secretary of State may issue guidance to the appropriate Agency with respect to the exercise or performance of that Agency's powers or duties under this Part; and in exercising or performing those powers or duties the appropriate Agency shall have regard to any such guidance so issued.

(2)   The duty imposed on the appropriate Agency by subsection (1) above is without prejudice to any duty imposed by any other provision of this Part on that Agency to act in accordance with guidance issued by the Secretary of State.

78X.   Supplementary provisions

(1)   Where it appears to a local authority that two or more different sites, when considered together, are in such a condition, by reason of substances in, on or under the land, that—

(a)   significant harm is being caused or there is a significant possibility of such harm being caused, or

(b)   pollution of controlled waters is being, or is likely to be, caused,

this Part shall apply in relation to each of those sites, whether or not the condition of the land at any of them, when considered alone, appears to the authority to be such that significant harm is being caused, or there is a significant possibility of such harm being caused, or that pollution of controlled waters is being or is likely to be caused.

(2)   Where it appears to a local authority that any land outside, but adjoining or adjacent to, its area is in such a condition, by reason of substances in, on or under the land, that significant harm is being caused, or there is a significant possibility of such harm being caused, or that pollution of controlled waters is being, or is likely to be, caused within its area—

(a)   the authority may, in exercising its functions under this Part, treat that land as if it were land situated within its area; and

(b)   except in this subsection, any reference—

    (i)   to land within the area of a local authority, or

    (ii)   to the local authority in whose area any land is situated,

shall be construed accordingly;

but this subsection is without prejudice to the functions of the local authority in whose area the land is in fact situated.

    (3)   A person acting in a relevant capacity—

    (a)   shall not thereby be personally liable, under this Part, to bear the whole or any part of the cost of doing any thing by way of remediation, unless that thing is to any extent referable to substances whose presence in, on or under the contaminated land in question is a result of any act done or omission made by him which it was unreasonable for a person acting in that capacity to do or make; and

    (b)   shall not thereby be guilty of an offence under or by virtue of section 78M above unless the requirement which has not been complied with is a requirement to do some particular thing for which he is personally liable to bear the whole or any part of the cost.

    (4)   In subsection (3) above, 'person acting in a relevant capacity' means—

    (a)   a person acting as an insolvency practitioner, within the meaning of section 388 of the Insolvency Act 1986 (including that section as it applies in relation to an insolvent partnership by virtue of any order made under section 421 of that Act);

    (b)   the official receiver acting in a capacity in which he would be regarded as acting as an insolvency practitioner within the meaning of section 388 of the Insolvency Act 1986 if subsection (5) of that section were disregarded;

    (c)   the official receiver acting as receiver or manager;

    (d)   a person acting as a special manager under section 177 or 370 of the Insolvency Act 1986;

    (e)   . . .

    (f)   a person acting as a receiver or receiver and manager—

    (i)   under or by virtue of any enactment; or

    (ii)   by virtue of his appointment as such by an order of a court or by any other instrument.

    (5)   Regulations may make different provision for different cases or circumstances.

78Y.   . . .

78YA.   Supplementary provisions with respect to guidance by the Secretary of State

    (1)   Any power of the Secretary of State to issue guidance under this Part shall only be exercisable after consultation with the appropriate Agency and such other bodies or persons as he may consider it appropriate to consult in relation to the guidance in question.

    (2)   A draft of any guidance proposed to be issued under section 78A(2) or (5), 78B(2) or 78F(6) or (7) above shall be laid before each House of Parliament and the guidance shall not be issued until after the period of 40 days beginning with the day

on which the draft was so laid or, if the draft is laid on different days, the later of the two days.

(3)   If, within the period mentioned in subsection (2) above, either House resolves that the guidance, the draft of which was laid before it, should not be issued, the Secretary of State shall not issue that guidance.

(4)   In reckoning any period of 40 days for the purposes of subsection (2) or (3) above, no account shall be taken of any time during which Parliament is dissolved or prorogued or during which both Houses are adjourned for more than four days.

(5)   The Secretary of State shall arrange for any guidance issued by him under this Part to be published in such manner as he considers appropriate.

78YB.   Interaction of this Part with other enactments

(1)   A remediation notice shall not be served if and to the extent that it appears to the enforcing authority that the powers of the appropriate Agency under section 27 above may be exercised in relation to—

(a)   the significant harm (if any), and

(b)   the pollution of controlled waters (if any),

by reason of which the contaminated land in question is such land.

(2)   Nothing in this Part shall apply in relation to any land in respect of which there is for the time being in force a site licence under Part II above, except to the extent that any significant harm, or pollution of controlled waters, by reason of which that land would otherwise fall to be regarded as contaminated land is attributable to causes other than—

(a)   breach of the conditions of the licence; or

(b)   the carrying on, in accordance with the conditions of the licence, of any activity authorised by the licence.

(3)   If, in a case falling within subsection (1) or (7) of section 59 above, the land in question is contaminated land, or becomes such land by reason of the deposit of the controlled waste in question, a remediation notice shall not be served in respect of that land by reason of that waste or any consequences of its deposit, if and to the extent that it appears to the enforcing authority that the powers of a waste regulation authority or waste collection authority under that section may be exercised in relation to that waste or the consequences of its deposit.

(4)   No remediation notice shall require a person to do anything the effect of which would be to impede or prevent the making of a discharge in pursuance of a consent given under Chapter II of Part III of the Water Resources Act 1991 (pollution offences) . . ..

78YC.   This Part and radioactivity

Except as provided by regulations, nothing in this Part applies in relation to harm, or pollution of controlled waters, so far as attributable to any radioactivity possessed by any substance; but regulations may—

(a)   provide for prescribed provisions of this Part to have effect with such modifications as the Secretary of State considers appropriate for the purpose of dealing with harm, or pollution of controlled waters, so far as attributable to any radioactivity possessed by any substances; or

    (b)   make such modifications of the Radioactive Substances Act 1993 or any other Act as the Secretary of State considers appropriate.

Appendix 2
Contaminated Land (England) Regulations 2000 (SI 2000 No. 227)

1. Citation, commencement, extent and interpretation

(1) These Regulations may be cited as the Contaminated Land (England) Regulations 2000 and shall come into force on l st April 2000.

(2) These Regulations extend to England only.

(3) In these Regulations, unless otherwise indicated, any reference to a numbered section is to the section of the Environmental Protection Act 1990 which bears that number.

2. Land required to be designated as a special site

(1) Contaminated land of the following descriptions is prescribed for the purposes of section 78C(8) as land required to be designated as a special site—

(a)　land to which regulation 3 applies;

(b)　land which is contaminated land by reason of waste acid tars in, on or under the land;

(c)　land on which any of the following activities have been carried on at any time—

(i)　the purification (including refining) of crude petroleum or of oil extracted from petroleum, shale or any other bituminous substance except coal; or

(ii)　the manufacture or processing of explosives;

(d)　land on which a prescribed process designated for central control has been or is being carried on under an authorisation where the process does not comprise solely things being done which are required by way of remediation;

(e)　land within a nuclear site;

(f)　land owned or occupied by or on behalf of—

(i)　the Secretary of State for Defence;

(ii)　the Defence Council;

(iii)　an international headquarters or defence organisation; or

(iv)　the service authority of a visiting force,

being land used for naval, military or air force purposes;

(g)　land on which the manufacture, production or disposal of—

(i)   chemical weapons;

(ii)   any biological agent or toxin which falls within section 1(1)(a) of the Biological Weapons Act 1974 (restriction on development of biological agents and toxins); or

(iii)   any weapon, equipment or means of delivery which falls within section 1(1)(b) of that Act (restriction on development of biological weapons), has been carried on at any time;

(h)   land comprising premises which are or were designated by the Secretary of State by an order made under section 1(1) of the Atomic Weapons Establishment Act 1991 (arrangements for development etc of nuclear devices);

(i)   land to which section 30 of the Armed Forces Act 1996 (land held for the benefit of Greenwich Hospital) applies; and

(j)   land which—

(i)   is adjoining or adjacent to land of a description specified in sub-paragraphs (b) to (i) above; and

(ii)   is contaminated land by virtue of substances which appear to have escaped from land of such a description.

(2)   For the purposes of paragraph (1)(b) above, 'waste acid tars' are tars which—

(a)   contain sulphuric acid;

(b)   were produced as a result of the refining of benzole, used lubricants or petroleum; and

(c)   are or were stored on land used as a retention basin for the disposal of such tars.

(3)   In paragraph (1)(d) above, 'authorisation' and 'prescribed process' have the same meaning as in Part I of the Environmental Protection Act 1990 (integrated pollution control and air pollution control by local authorities) and the reference to designation for central control is a reference to designation under section 2(4) (which provides for processes to be designated for central or local control).

(4)   In paragraph (1)(e) above, 'nuclear site' means—

(a)   any site in respect of which, or part of which, a nuclear site licence is for the time being in force; or

(b)   any site in respect of which, or part of which, after the revocation or surrender of a nuclear site licence, the period of responsibility of the licensee has not come to an end;

and 'nuclear site licence', 'licensee' and 'period of responsibility' have the meaning given by the Nuclear Installations Act 1965.

(5)   For the purposes of paragraph (1)(f) above, land used for residential purposes or by the Navy, Army and Air Force Institutes shall be treated as land used for naval, military or air force purposes only if the land forms part of a base occupied for naval, military or air force purposes.

(6)   In paragraph (1)(f) above—

'international headquarters' and 'defence organisation' mean, respectively, any international headquarters or defence organisation designated for the purposes of the International Headquarters and Defence Organisations Act 1964;

'service authority' and 'visiting force' have the same meaning as in Part I of the Visiting Forces Act 1952.

(7)   In paragraph (1)(g) above, 'chemical weapon' has the same meaning as in subsection (1) of section 1 of the Chemical Weapons Act 1996 disregarding subsection (2) of that section.

3.   Pollution of controlled waters

For the purposes of regulation 2(1)(a), this regulation applies to land where—

(a)   controlled waters which are, or are intended to be, used for the supply of drinking water for human consumption are being affected by the land and, as a result, require a treatment process or a change in such a process to be applied to those waters before use, so as to be regarded as wholesome within the meaning of Part III of the Water Industry Act 1991 (water supply);

(b)   controlled waters are being affected by the land and, as a result, those waters do not meet or are not likely to meet the criterion for classification applying to the relevant description of waters specified in regulations made under section 82 of the Water Resources Act 1991 (classification of quality of waters); or

(c)   controlled waters are being affected by the land and—

(i)   any of the substances by reason of which the pollution of the waters is being or is likely to be caused falls within any of the families or groups of substances listed in paragraph 1 of Schedule 1 to these Regulations; and

(ii)   the waters, or any part of the waters, are contained within underground strata which comprise wholly or partly any of the formations of rocks listed in paragraph 2 of Schedule 1 to these Regulations.

4.   Content of remediation notices

(1)   A remediation notice shall state (in addition to the matters required by section 78E(1) and (3))—

(a)   the name and address of the person on whom the notice is served;

(b)   the location and extent of the contaminated land to which the notice relates (in this regulation referred to as the 'contaminated land in question'), sufficient to enable it to be identified whether by reference to a plan or otherwise;

(c)   the date of any notice which was given under section 78B to the person on whom the remediation notice is served identifying the contaminated land in question as contaminated land;

(d)   whether the enforcing authority considers the person on whom the notice is served is an appropriate person by reason of—

(i)   having caused or knowingly permitted the substances, or any of the substances, by reason of which the contaminated land in question is contaminated land, to be in, on or under that land;

(ii)   being the owner of the contaminated land in question; or

(iii)   being the occupier of the contaminated land in question;

(e)   particulars of the significant harm or pollution of controlled waters by reason of which the contaminated land in question is contaminated land,

(f)   the substances by reason of which the contaminated land in question is contaminated land and, if any of the substances have escaped from other land, the location of that other land;

(g)   the enforcing authority's reasons for its decisions as to the things by way of remediation that the appropriate person is required to do, which shall show how any guidance issued by the Secretary of State under section 78E(5) has been applied;

(h)   where two or more persons are appropriate persons in relation to the contaminated land in question—

(i)   that this is the case;

(ii)   the name and address of each such person; and

(iii)   the thing by way of remediation for which each such person bears responsibility;

(i)   where two or more persons would, apart from section 78F(6), be appropriate persons in relation to any particular thing which is to be done by way of remediation, the enforcing authority's reasons for its determination as to whether any, and if so which, of them is to be treated as not being an appropriate person in relation to that thing, which shall show how any guidance issued by the Secretary of State under section 78F(6) has been applied;

(j)   where the remediation notice is required by section 78E(3) to state the proportion of the cost of a thing which is to be done by way of remediation which each of the appropriate persons in relation to that thing is liable to bear, the enforcing authority's reasons for the proportion which it has determined, which shall show how any guidance issued by the Secretary of State under section 78F(7) has been applied;

(k)   where known to the enforcing authority, the name and address of—

(i)   the owner of the contaminated land in question; and

(ii)   any person who appears to the enforcing authority to be in occupation of the whole or any part of the contaminated land in question;

(l)   where known to the enforcing authority, the name and address of any person whose consent is required under section 78G(2) before any thing required by the remediation notice may be done;

(m)   where the notice is to be served in reliance on section 78H(4), that it appears to the enforcing authority that the contaminated land in question is in such a condition, by reason of substances in, on or under the land, that there is imminent danger of serious harm, or serious pollution of controlled waters, being caused;

(n)   that a person on whom a remediation notice is served may be guilty of an offence for failure, without reasonable excuse, to comply with any of the requirements of the notice;

(o)   the penalties which may be applied on conviction for such an offence;

(p)   the name and address of the enforcing authority serving the notice; and

(q)   the date of the notice.

(2)   A remediation notice shall explain—

(a)   that a person on whom it is served has a right of appeal against the notice under section 78L;

(b)   how, within what period and on what grounds an appeal may be made; and

(c)   that a notice is suspended, where an appeal is duly made, until the final determination or abandonment of the appeal.

5.   Service of copies of remediation notices

(1)   Subject to paragraph (2) below, the enforcing authority shall, at the same time as it serves a remediation notice, send a copy of it to each of the following persons, not being a person on whom the notice is to be served—

(a)   any person who was required to be consulted under section 78G(3) before service of the notice;

(b)   any person who was required to be consulted under section 78H(1) before service of the notice;

(c)   where the local authority is the enforcing authority, the Environment Agency; and

(d)   where the Environment Agency is the enforcing authority, the local authority in whose area the contaminated land in question is situated.

(2)   Where it appears to the enforcing authority that the contaminated land in question is in such a condition by reason of substances in, on or under it that there is imminent danger of serious harm, or serious pollution of controlled waters, being caused, the enforcing authority shall send any copies of the notice pursuant to paragraph (1) above as soon as practicable after service of the notice.

6.   Compensation for rights of entry etc.

Schedule 2 to these Regulations shall have effect—

(a)   for prescribing the period within which a person who grants, or joins in granting, any rights pursuant to section 78G(2) may apply for compensation for the grant of those rights;   ·

(b)   for prescribing the manner in which, and the person to whom, such an application may be made; and

(c)   for prescribing the manner in which the amount of such compensation shall be determined and for making further provision relating to such compensation.

7.   Grounds of appeal against a remediation notice

(1)   The grounds of appeal against a remediation notice under section 78L(1) are any of the following—

(a)   that, in determining whether any land to which the notice relates appears to be contaminated land, the local authority—

(i)   failed to act in accordance with guidance issued by the Secretary of State under section 78A(2), (5) or (6); or

(ii)   whether by reason of such a failure or otherwise, unreasonably identified all or any of the land to which the notice relates as contaminated land;

(b)   that, in determining a requirement of the notice, the enforcing authority—

(i)   failed to have regard to guidance issued by the Secretary of State under section 78E(5); or

(ii)   whether by reason of such a failure or otherwise, unreasonably required the appellant to do any thing by way of remediation;

(c)   that the enforcing authority unreasonably determined the appellant to be the appropriate, person who is to bear responsibility for any thing required by the notice to be done by way of remediation;

(d)   subject to paragraph (2) below, that the enforcing authority unreasonably failed to determine that some person in addition to the appellant is an appropriate person in relation to any thing required by the notice to be done by way of remediation;

(e)   that, in respect of any thing required by the notice to be done by way of remediation, the enforcing authority failed to act in accordance with guidance issued by the Secretary of State under section 78F(6);

(f)   that, where two or more persons are appropriate persons in relation to any thing required by the notice to be done by way of remediation, the enforcing authority—

(i)   failed to determine the proportion of the cost stated in the notice to be the liability of the appellant in accordance with guidance issued by the Secretary of State under section 78F(7); or

(ii)   whether, by reason of such a failure or otherwise, unreasonably determined the proportion of the cost that the appellant is to bear,

(g)   that service of the notice contravened a provision of subsection (1) or (3) of section 78H (restrictions and prohibitions on serving remediation notices) other than in circumstances where section 78H(4) applies;

(h)   that, where the notice was served in reliance on section 78H(4) without compliance with section 78H(1) or (3), the enforcing authority could not reasonably have taken the view that the contaminated land in question was in such a condition by reason of substances in, on or under the land, that there was imminent danger of serious harm, or serious pollution of controlled waters, being caused;

(i)   that the enforcing authority has unreasonably failed to be satisfied, in accordance with section 78H(5)(b), that appropriate things are being, or will be, done by way of remediation without service of a notice;

(j)   that any thing required by the notice to be done by way of remediation was required in contravention of a provision of section 78J (restrictions on liability relating to the pollution of controlled waters);

(k)   that any thing required by the notice to be done by way of remediation was required in contravention of a provision of section 78K (liability in respect of contaminating substances which escape to other land);

(l)   that the enforcing authority itself has power, in a case falling within section 78N(3)(b), to do what is appropriate by way of remediation;

(m)   that the enforcing authority itself has power, in a case falling within section 78N(3)(e), to do what is appropriate by way of remediation;

(n)   that the enforcing authority, in considering for the purposes of section 78N(3)(e), whether it would seek to recover all or a portion of the cost incurred by it in doing some particular thing by way of remediation—

(i)   failed to have regard to any hardship which the recovery may cause to the person from whom the cost is recoverable or to any guidance issued by the Secretary of State for the purposes of section 78P(2); or

(ii)   whether by reason of such a failure or otherwise, unreasonably determined that it would decide to seek to recover all of the cost;

(o)   that, in determining a requirement of the notice, the enforcing authority failed to have regard to guidance issued by the Environment Agency under section 78V(1);

(p)   that a period specified in the notice within which the appellant is required to do anything is not reasonably sufficient for the purpose;

(q)   that the notice provides for a person acting in a relevant capacity to be personally liable to bear the whole or part of the cost of doing any thing by way of remediation, contrary to the provisions of section 78X(3)(a);

(r)   that service of the notice contravened a provision of section 78YB (interaction of Part IIA of the Environmental Protection Act 1990 with other enactments), and—

(i)   in a case where subsection (1) of that section is relied on, that it ought reasonably to have appeared to the enforcing authority that the powers of the Environment Agency under section 27 might be exercised;

(ii)   in a case where subsection (3) of section 78YB is relied on, that it ought reasonably to have appeared to the enforcing authority that the powers of a waste regulation authority or waste collection authority under section 59 might be exercised; or

(s)   that there has been some informality, defect or error in, or in connection with, the notice, in respect of which there is no right of appeal under the grounds set out in sub-paragraphs (a) to (r) above.

(2)   A person may only appeal on the ground specified in paragraph (1)(d) above in a case where—

(a)   the enforcing authority has determined that he is an appropriate person by virtue of subsection (2) of section 78F and he claims to have found some other person who is an appropriate person by virtue of that subsection;

(b)   the notice is served on him as the owner or occupier for the time being of the contaminated land in question and he claims to have found some other person who is an appropriate person by virtue of that subsection; or

(c)   the notice is served on him as the owner or occupier for the time being of the contaminated land in question, and he claims that some other person is also an owner or occupier for the time being of the whole or part of that land.

(3)   If and in so far as an appeal against a remediation notice is based on the ground of some informality, defect or error in, or in connection with, the notice, the appellate authority shall dismiss the appeal if it is satisfied that the informality, defect or error was not a material one.

8.   Appeals to a magistrates' court

(1)   An appeal under section 78L(1) to a magistrates' court against a remediation notice shall be by way of complaint for an order and, subject to section 78L(2) and (3) and regulations 7(3), 12 and 13, the Magistrates' Courts Act 1980 shall apply to the proceedings.

(2)   An appellant shall, at the same time as he makes a complaint,—

    (a)   file a notice ('notice of appeal') and serve a copy of it on—

        (i)   the enforcing authority;

        (ii)   any person named in the remediation notice as an appropriate person;

        (iii)   any person named in the notice of appeal as an appropriate person; and

        (iv)   any person named in the remediation notice as the owner or occupier of the whole or any part of the land to which the notice relates;

    (b)   file a copy of the remediation notice to which the appeal relates and serve a copy of it on any person named in the notice of appeal as an appropriate person who was not so named in the remediation notice; and

    (c)   file a statement of the names and addresses of any persons falling within paragraph (ii), (iii) or (iv) of sub-paragraph (a) above.

(3)   The notice of appeal shall state the appellant's name and address and the grounds on which the appeal is made.

(4)   On an appeal under section 78L(1) to a magistrates' court—

    (a)   the justices' clerk or the court may give, vary or revoke directions for the conduct of proceedings, including—

        (i)   the timetable for the proceedings;

        (ii)   the service of documents;

        (iii)   the submission of evidence; and

        (iv)   the order of speeches;

    (b)   any person falling within paragraph (2)(a)(ii), (iii) or (iv) above shall be given notice of, and an opportunity to be heard at, the hearing of the complaint and any hearing for directions, in addition to the appellant and the enforcing authority; and

    (c)   the court may refuse to grant a request by the appellant to abandon his appeal against a remediation notice, where the request is made after the court has notified the appellant in accordance with regulation 12(1) of a proposed modification of that notice.

(5)   Rule 15 of the Family Proceedings Courts (Matrimonial Proceedings etc.) Rules 1991 (delegation by justices' clerk) shall apply for the purposes of an appeal under section 78L(1) to a magistrates' court as it applies for the purposes of Part II of those Rules.

(6)   In this regulation, 'file' means deposit with the justices' clerk.

9.   Appeals to the Secretary of State

(1)   An appeal to the Secretary of State against a remediation notice shall be made to him by a notice ('notice of appeal') which shall state—

    (a)   the name and address of the appellant;

    (b)   the grounds on which the appeal is made; and

    (c)   whether the appellant wishes the appeal to be in the form of a hearing or to be disposed of on the basis of written representations.

(2)   The appellant shall, at the same time as he serves a notice of appeal on the Secretary of State,—

   (a)   serve a copy of it on—

      (i)   the Environment Agency;

     (ii)   any person named in the remediation notice as an appropriate person;

   (iii)   any person named in the notice of appeal as an appropriate person; and

   (iv)   any person named in the remediation notice as the owner or occupier
of the whole or any part of the land to which the notice relates;
and serve on the Secretary of State a statement of the names and addresses of any
persons falling within paragraph (ii), (iii) or (iv) above;and

   (b)   serve a copy of the remediation notice to which the appeal relates on the
Secretary of State and on any person named in the notice of appeal as an appropriate
person who is not so named in the remediation notice.

   (3)   Subject to paragraph (5) below, if the appellant wishes to abandon an appeal,
he shall do so by notifying the Secretary of State in writing and the appeal shall be
treated as abandoned on the date the Secretary of State receives that notification.

   (4)   The Secretary of State may refuse to permit an appellant to abandon his
appeal against a remediation notice where the notification by the appellant in
accordance with paragraph (3) above is received by the Secretary of State at any time
after the Secretary of State has notified the appellant in accordance with regulation
12(1) of a proposed modification of that notice.

   (5)   Where an appeal is abandoned, the Secretary of State shall give notice of the
abandonment to any person on whom the appellant was required to serve a copy of
the notice of appeal.

10.   Hearings and local inquiries

   (1)   Before determining an appeal, the Secretary of State may, if he thinks fit—

   (a)   cause the appeal to take or continue in the form of a hearing (which may,
if the person hearing the appeal so decides, be held, or held to any extent, in private);
or

   (b)   cause a local inquiry to be held,
and the Secretary of State shall act as mentioned in sub-paragraph (a) or (b) above if
a request is made by either the appellant or the Environment Agency to be heard with
respect to the appeal.

   (2)   The persons entitled to be heard at a hearing are—

   (a)   the appellant

   (b)   the Environment Agency; and

   (c)   any person (other than the Agency) on whom the appellant was required
to serve a copy of the notice of appeal.

   (3)   Nothing in paragraph (2) above shall prevent the person appointed to conduct
the hearing of the appeal from permitting any other person to be heard at the hearing
and such permission shall not be unreasonably withheld.

   (4)   After the conclusion of a hearing, the person appointed to conduct the hearing
shall, unless he has been appointed under section 114(1)(a) of the Environment Act
1995 (power of Secretary of State to delegate his functions of determining appeals)
to determine the appeal, make a report in writing to the Secretary of State which shall

include his conclusions and his recommendations or his reasons for not making any recommendations.

11. Notification of Secretary of State's decision on an appeal

(1) The Secretary of State shall notify the appellant in writing of his decision on an appeal and shall provide him with a copy of any report mentioned in regulation 10(4).

(2) The Secretary of State shall, at the same time as he notifies the appellant, send a copy of the documents mentioned in paragraph (1) above to the Environment Agency and to any other person on whom the appellant was required to serve a copy of the notice of appeal.

12. Modification of a remediation notice

(1) Before modifying a remediation notice under section 78L(2)(b) in any respect which would be less favourable to the appellant or any other person on whom the notice was served, the appellate authority shall—

(a) notify the appellant and any persons on whom the appellant was required to serve a copy of the notice of appeal of the proposed modification;

(b) permit any persons so notified to make representations in relation to the proposed modification; and

(c) permit the appellant or any other person on whom the remediation notice was served to be heard if any such person so requests.

(2) Where, in accordance with paragraph (1) above, the appellant or any other person is heard, the enforcing authority shall also be entitled to be heard.

13. Appeals to the High Court

An appeal against any decision of a magistrates' court in pursuance of an appeal under section 78L(1) shall lie to the High Court at the instance of any party to the proceedings in which the decision was given (including any person who exercised his entitlement under regulation 8(4)(b) to be heard at the hearing of the complaint).

14. Suspension of a remediation notice

(1) Where an appeal is duly made against a remediation notice, the notice shall be of no effect pending the final determination or abandonment of the appeal.

(2) An appeal against a remediation notice is duly made for the purposes of this regulation if it is made within the period specified in section 78L(1) and the requirements of regulation 8(2) and (3) (in the case of an appeal to a magistrates' court) or regulation 9(1) and (2) (in the case of an appeal to the Secretary of State) have been complied with.

15. Registers

(1) Schedule 3 to these Regulations shall have effect for prescribing—

(a) for the purposes of subsection (1) of section 78R, the particulars of or relating to the matters to be contained in a register maintained under that section; and

(b) other matters in respect of which such a register shall contain prescribed particulars pursuant to section 78R(1)(l).

(2)   The following descriptions of information are prescribed for the purposes of section 78R(2) as information to be contained in notifications for the purposes of section 78R(1)(h) and (j)—

    (a)   the location and extent of the land sufficient to enable it to be identified;

    (b)   the name and address of the person who it is claimed has done each of the things by way of remediation;

    (c)   a description of any thing which it is claimed has been done by way of remediation; and

    (d)   the period within which it is claimed each such thing was done.

(3)   The following places are prescribed for the purposes of subsection (8) of section 78R as places at which any registers or facilities for obtaining copies shall be available or afforded to the public in pursuance of paragraph (a) or (b) of that subsection—

    (a)   where the enforcing authority is the local authority, its principal office; and

    (b)   where the enforcing authority is the Environment Agency, its office for the area in which the contaminated land in question is situated.

Signed by authority of the Secretary of State

Michael Meacher
Minister of State,
Department of the Environment,
Transport and the Regions

2nd February 2000

Regulation 3(c)   SCHEDULE 1

SPECIAL SITES

1.   The following families and groups of substances are listed for the purposes of regulation 3(c)(i)—

organohalogen compounds and substances which may form such compounds in the aquatic environment;

organophosphorus compounds;

organotin compounds;

substances which possess carcinogenic, mutagenic or teratogenic properties in or via the aquatic environment;

mercury and its compounds;

cadmium and its compounds;

mineral oil and other hydrocarbons;

cyanides.

2.   The following formations of rocks are listed for the purposes of regulation 3(c)(ii)—

Pleistocene Norwich Crag;

Upper Cretaceous Chalk;

Lower Cretaceous Sandstones;
Upper Jurassic Corallian;
Middle Jurassic Limestones;
Lower Jurassic Cotteswold Sands;
Permo-Triassic Sherwood Sandstone Group;
Upper Permian Magnesian Limestone;
Lower Permian Penrith Sandstone;
Lower Permian Collyhurst Sandstone;
Lower Permian Basal Breccias, Conglomerates and Sandstones;
Lower Carboniferous Limestones.

Regulation 6   SCHEDULE 2

COMPENSATION FOR RIGHTS OF ENTRY ETC.

Interpretation

1.   In this Schedule—
'the 1961 Act' means the Land Compensation Act 1961
'grantor' means a person who has granted, or joined in the granting of, any rights
pursuant to section 78G(2);
'relevant interest' means an interest in land out of which rights have been granted
pursuant to section 78G(2).

Period for making an application

2.   An application for compensation shall be made within the period beginning
with the date of the grant of the rights in respect of which compensation is claimed
and ending on whichever is the latest of the following dates—

(a)   twelve months after the date of the grant of those rights;

(b)   where an appeal is made against a remediation notice in respect of which
the rights in question have been granted, and the notice is of no effect by virtue of
regulation 14, twelve months after the date of the final determination or abandonment
of the appeal; or

(c)   six months after the date on which the rights were first exercised.

Manner of making an application

3.—(1)   An application shall be made in writing and delivered at or sent by
pre-paid post to the last known address for correspondence of the appropriate person
to whom the rights were granted.

(2)   The application shall contain, or be accompanied by—

(a)   a copy of the grant of rights in respect of which the grantor is applying for
compensation, and of any plans attached to that grant;

(b)   a description of the exact nature of any interest in land in respect of which
compensation is applied for, and

(c)   a statement of the amount of compensation applied for, distinguishing the
amounts applied for under each of sub-paragraphs (a) to (e) of paragraph 4 below,

and showing how the amount applied for under each sub-paragraph has been calculated.

Loss and damage for which compensation payable

4.   Subject to paragraph 5(3) and (5)(b) below, compensation is payable under section 78G for loss and damage of the following descriptions—

(a)   depreciation in the value of any relevant interest to which the grantor is entitled which results from the grant of the rights;

(b)   depreciation in the value of any other interest in land to which the grantor is entitled which results from the exercise of the rights;

(c)   loss or damage, in relation to any relevant interest to which the grantor is entitled, which—

(i)   is attributable to the grant of the rights or the exercise of them;

(ii)   does not consist of depreciation in the value of that interest; and

(iii)   is loss or damage for which he would have been entitled to compensation by way of compensation for disturbance, if that interest had been acquired compulsorily under the Acquisition of Land Act 1981 in pursuance of a notice to treat served on the date on which the rights were granted;

(d)   damage to, or injurious affection of, any interest in land to which the grantor is entitled which is not a relevant interest, and which results from the grant of the rights or the exercise of them; and

(e)   loss in respect of work carried out by or on behalf of the grantor which is rendered abortive by the grant of the rights or the exercise of them.

Basis on which compensation assessed

5.—(1)   The following provisions shall have effect for the purpose of assessing the amount to be paid by way of compensation under section 78G.

(2)   The rules set out in section 5 of the 1961 Act (rules for assessing compensation) shall, so far as applicable and subject to any necessary modifications, have effect for the purpose of assessing any such compensation as they have effect for the purpose of assessing compensation for the compulsory acquisition of an interest in land.

(3)   No account shall be taken of any enhancement of the value of any interest in land, by reason of any building erected, work done or improvement or alteration made on any land in which the grantor is, or was at the time of erection, doing or making, directly or indirectly concerned, if the Lands Tribunal is satisfied that the erection of the building, the doing of the work, the making of the improvement or the alteration was not reasonably necessary and was undertaken with a view to obtaining compensation or increased compensation.

(4)   In calculating the amount of any loss under paragraph 4(e) above, expenditure incurred in the preparation of plans or on other similar preparatory matters shall be taken into account.

(5)   Where the interest in respect of which compensation is to be assessed is subject to a mortgage—

(a)   the compensation shall be assessed as if the interest were not subject to the mortgage; and

(b)   no compensation shall be payable in respect of the interest of the mortgagee (as distinct from the interest which is subject to the mortgage).

(6)   Compensation under section 78G shall include an amount equal to the grantor's reasonable valuation and legal expenses.

Payment of compensation and determination of disputes

6.—(1)   Compensation payable under section 78G in respect of an interest which is subject to a mortgage shall be paid to the mortgagee or, if there is more than one mortgagee, to the first mortgagee and shall, in either case, be applied by him as if it were proceeds of sale.

(2)   Amounts of compensation determined under this Schedule shall be payable—

(a)   where the appropriate person and the grantor or mortgagee agree that a single payment is to be made on a specified date, on that date;

(b)   where the appropriate person and the grantor or mortgagee agree that payment is to be made in instalments at different dates, on the date agreed as regards each instalment; and

(c)   in any other case, subject to any direction of the Lands Tribunal or the court, as soon as reasonably practicable after the amount of the compensation has been finally determined.

(3)   Any question of the application of paragraph 5(3) above or of disputed compensation shall be referred to and determined by the Lands Tribunal.

(4)   In relation to the determination of any such question, sections 2 and 4 of the 1961 Act (procedure on reference to the Lands Tribunal and costs) shall apply as if—

(a)   the reference in section 2(1) of that Act to section 1 of that Act were a reference to sub-paragraph (3) of this paragraph; and

(b)   references in section 4 of that Act to the acquiring authority were references to the appropriate person.

Regulation 15   SCHEDULE 3

REGISTERS

A register maintained by an enforcing authority under section 78R shall contain full particulars of the following matters—

Remediation notices

1.   In relation to a remediation notice served by the authority—

(a)   the name and address of the person on whom the notice is served;

(b)   the location and extent of the contaminated land to which the notice relates (in this paragraph referred to as the 'contaminated land in question'), sufficient to enable it to be identified whether by reference to a plan or otherwise;

(c)   the significant harm or pollution of controlled waters by reason of which the contaminated land in question is contaminated land;

(d)   the substances by reason of which the contaminated land in question is contaminated land and, if any of the substances have escaped from other land, the location of that other land;

(e)   the current use of the contaminated land in question;

(f)   what each appropriate person is to do by way of remediation and the periods within which they are required to do each of the things; and

(g)   the date of the notice.

Appeals against remediation notices

2.   Any appeal against a remediation notice served by the authority.

3.   Any decision on such an appeal.

Remediation declarations

4.   Any remediation declaration prepared and published by the enforcing authority under section 78H(6).

5.   In relation to any such remediation declaration—

(a)   the location and extent of the contaminated land in question, sufficient to enable it to be identified whether by reference to a plan or otherwise; and

(b)   the matters referred to in sub-paragraphs (c), (d) and (e) of paragraph 1 above.

Remediation statements

6.   Any remediation statement prepared and published by the responsible person under section 78H(7) or by the enforcing authority under section 78H (9).

7.   In relation to any such remediation statement—

(a)   the location and extent of the contaminated land in question, sufficient to enable it to be identified whether by reference to a plan or otherwise; and

(b)   the matters referred to in sub-paragraphs (c), (d) and (e) of paragraph 1 above.

Appeals against charging notices

8.   In the case of an enforcing authority, any appeal under section 78P(8) against a charging notice served by the authority.

9.   Any decision on such an appeal.

Designation of special sites

10.   In the case of the Environment Agency, as respects any land in relation to which it is the enforcing authority, and in the case of a local authority, as respects any land in its area,—

(a)   any notice given by a local authority under subsection (1)(b) or (5)(a) of section 78C, or by the Secretary of State under section 78D(4)(b), which, by virtue of section 78C(7) or section 78D(6) respectively, has effect as the designation of any land as a special site;

(b)   the provisions of regulation 2 or 3 by virtue of which the land is required to be designated as a special site;

(c)   any notice given by the Environment Agency under section 78Q(1)(a) of its decision to adopt a remediation notice; and

(d)   any notice given by or to the enforcing authority under section 78Q(4) terminating the designation of any land as a special site.

Notification of claimed remediation

11.   Any notification given to the authority for the purposes of section 78R (1)(h) or (j).

Convictions for offences under section 78M

12.   Any conviction of a person for any offence under section 78M in relation to a remediation notice served by the authority, including the name of the offender, the date of conviction, the penalty imposed and the name of the Court.

Guidance issued under section 78V(1)

13.   In the case of the Environment Agency, the date of any guidance issued by it under subsection (1) of section 78V and, in the case of a local authority, the date of any guidance issued by the Agency to it under that subsection.

Other environmental controls

14.   Where the authority is precluded by virtue of section 78YB(1) from serving a remediation notice—

(a)   the location and extent of the contaminated land in question, sufficient to enable it to be identified whether by reference to a plan or otherwise;

(b)   the matters referred to in sub-paragraphs (c), (d) and (e) of paragraph 1 above; and

(c)   any steps of which the authority has knowledge, carried out under section 27, towards remedying any significant harm or pollution of controlled waters by reason of which the land in question is contaminated land.

15.   Where the authority is precluded by virtue of section 78YB(3) from serving a remediation notice in respect of land which is contaminated land by reason of the deposit of controlled waste or any consequences of its deposit—

(a)   the location and extent of the contaminated land in question, sufficient to enable it to be identified whether by reference to a plan or otherwise;

(b)   the matters referred to in sub-paragraphs (c), (d) and (e) of paragraph 1 above; and

(c)   any steps of which the authority has knowledge, carried out under section 59, in relation to that waste or the consequences of its deposit, including in a case where a waste collection authority (within the meaning of section 30(3)) took those steps or required the steps to be taken, the name of that authority.

16.   Where, as a result of a consent given under Chapter II of Part III of the Water Resources Act 1991 (pollution offences), the authority is precluded by virtue of section 78YB(4) from specifying in a remediation notice any particular thing by way of remediation which it would otherwise have specified in such a notice,—

    (a)   the consent;

    (b)   the location and extent of the contaminated land in question, sufficient to enable it to be identified whether by reference to a plan or otherwise; and

    (c)   the matters referred to in sub-paragraphs (c), (d) and (e) of paragraph 1 above.

Appendix 3
Department of the Environment, Transport and the Regions Circular on Contaminated Land

ANNEX 3

CHAPTER A — STATUTORY GUIDANCE ON THE DEFINITION OF CONTAMINATED LAND

PART 1   SCOPE OF THE CHAPTER

A.1   The statutory guidance in this Chapter is issued under section 78A(2), (5) and (6) of Part IIA of the Environmental Protection Act 1990 and provides guidance on applying the definition of contaminated land.

A.2   'Contaminated land' is defined at section 78A(2) as:

'any land which appears to the local authority in whose area it is situated to be in such a condition, by reason of substances in, on or under the land, that—

(a)   significant harm is being caused or there is a significant possibility of such harm being caused; or

(b)   pollution of controlled waters is being, or is likely to be caused; . . .'

A.3   Section 78A(5) further provides that:

'the questions—

(a)   what harm is to be regarded as 'significant'

(b)   whether the possibility of significant harm being caused is 'significant'

(c)   whether pollution of controlled waters is being, or is likely to be caused,

shall be determined in accordance with guidance issued . . . by the Secretary of State'.

A.4   In determining these questions the local authority is therefore required to act in accordance with the guidance contained in this Chapter.

A.5   As well as defining contaminated land, section 78A(2) further provides that:

'. . . in determining whether any land appears to be such land, a local authority shall . . . act in accordance with guidance issued by the Secretary of State . . . with respect to the manner in which that determination is to be made'

A.6   Guidance on the manner in which that determination is to be made is set out in Part 3 of the statutory guidance in Chapter B.

PART 2   DEFINITIONS OF TERMS AND GENERAL MATERIAL

A.7   Unless otherwise stated, any word, term or phrase given a specific meaning in Part IIA of the Environmental Protection Act 1990 has the same meaning for the purposes of the guidance in this Chapter.

A.8   Any reference to 'Part IIA' means 'Part IIA of the Environmental Protection Act 1990'. Any reference to a 'section' in primary legislation means a section of the Environmental Protection Act 1990, unless it is specifically stated otherwise.

RISK ASSESSMENT

A.9   The definition of contaminated land is based upon the principles of risk assessment. For the purposes of this guidance, 'risk' is defined as the combination of:

(a)   the probability, or frequency, of occurrence of a defined hazard (for example, exposure to a property of a substance with the potential to cause harm); and

(b)   the magnitude (including the seriousness) of the consequences.

A.10   The guidance below follows established approaches to risk assessment, including the concept of contaminant-pathway-receptor. (In the technical literature, this is sometimes referred to as source-pathway-target.)

A.11   There are two steps in applying the definition of contaminated land. The first step is for the local authority to satisfy itself that a 'contaminant', a 'pathway' (or pathways), and a 'receptor' have been identified with respect to that land. These three concepts are defined for the purposes of this Chapter in paragraphs A.12 to A.14 below.

A.12   A contaminant is a substance which is in, on or under the land and which has the potential to cause harm or to cause pollution of controlled waters.

A.13   A receptor is either:

(a)   a living organism, a group of living organisms, an ecological system or a piece of property which

(i)   is in a category listed in Table A (see below) as a type of receptor, and

(ii)   is being, or could be, harmed, by a contaminant; or

(b)   controlled waters which are being, or could be, polluted by a contaminant.

A.14   A pathway is one or more routes or means by, or through, which a receptor:

(a)   is being exposed to, or affected by, a contaminant, or

(b)   could be so exposed or affected.

A.15   It is possible for a pathway to be identified for this purpose on the basis of a reasonable assessment of the general scientific knowledge about the nature of a particular contaminant and of the circumstances of the land in question. Direct observation of the pathway is not necessary.

A.16   The identification of each of these three elements is linked to the identification of the others. A pathway can only be identified if it is capable of exposing an identified receptor to an identified contaminant. That particular contaminant should likewise be capable of harming or, in the case of controlled waters, be capable of polluting that particular receptor.

A.17   In this Chapter, a 'pollutant linkage' means the relationship between a contaminant, a pathway and a receptor, and a 'pollutant' means the contaminant in a pollutant linkage. Unless all three elements of a pollutant linkage are identified in respect of a piece of land, that land should not be identified as contaminated land. There may be more than one pollutant linkage on any given piece of land.

A.18   For the purposes of determining whether a pollutant linkage exists (and for describing any such linkage), the local authority may treat two or more substances as being a single substance, in any case where:

(a)   the substances are compounds of the same element, or have similar molecular structures; and

(b)   it is the presence of that element, or the particular type of molecular structures, that determines the effect that the substances may have on the receptor which forms part of the pollutant linkage.

A.19   The second step in applying the definition of contaminated land is for the local authority to satisfy itself that both:

(a)   such a pollutant linkage exists in respect of a piece of land; and

(b)   that pollutant linkage:

(i)   is resulting in significant harm being caused to the receptor in the pollutant linkage,

(ii)   presents a significant possibility of significant harm being caused to that receptor,

(iii)   is resulting in the pollution of the controlled waters which constitute the receptor, or

(iv)   is likely to result in such pollution.

A.20   In this Chapter, a 'significant pollutant linkage' means a pollutant linkage which forms the basis for a determination that a piece of land is contaminated land. A 'significant pollutant' is a pollutant in a 'significant pollutant linkage'.

A.21   The guidance in Part 3 below relates to questions about significant harm and the significant possibility of such harm being caused. The guidance in Part 4 below relates to the pollution of controlled waters.

PART 3   SIGNIFICANT HARM AND THE SIGNIFICANT POSSIBILITY OF SIGNIFICANT HARM

A.22   Section 78A(4) defines 'harm' as meaning 'harm to the health of living organisms or other interference with the ecological systems of which they form part and, in the case of man, includes harm to his property'. Section 78A(5) provides that what harm is to be regarded as 'significant' and whether the possibility of significant harm being caused is significant shall be determined in accordance with this guidance.

WHAT HARM IS TO BE REGARDED AS 'SIGNIFICANT'

A.23   The local authority should regard as significant only harm which is both:

(a)   to a receptor of a type listed in Table A, and

(b)   within the description of harm specified for that type of receptor in that Table.

A.24   The local authority should not regard harm to receptors of any type other than those mentioned in Table A as being significant harm for the purposes of Part IIA. For example, harm to ecological systems outside the descriptions in the second entry in the table should be disregarded. Similarly, the authority should not regard any other description of harm to receptors of the types mentioned in Table A as being significant harm.

A.25   The authority should disregard any receptors which are not likely to be present, given the 'current use' of the land or other land which might be affected.

A.26   For the purposes of this guidance, the 'current use' means any use which is currently being made, or is likely to be made, of the land and which is consistent with any existing planning permission (or is otherwise lawful under town and country planning legislation). This definition is subject to the following qualifications:

(a)   the current use should be taken to include any temporary use, permitted under town and country planning legislation, to which the land is, or is likely to be, put from time to time;

(b)   the current use includes future uses or developments which do not require a new, or amended, grant of planning permission (but see also paragraph A.34 below);

(c)   the current use should, nevertheless, be taken to include any likely informal recreational use of the land, whether authorised by the owners or occupiers or not, (for example, children playing on the land); however, in assessing the likelihood of any such informal use, the local authority should give due attention to measures taken to prevent or restrict access to the land; and

(d)   in the case of agricultural land, however, the current agricultural use should not be taken to extend beyond the growing or rearing of the crops or animals which are habitually grown or reared on the land.

Table A — Categories of Significant Harm

Type of Receptor	Description of harm to that type of receptor that is to be regarded as significant harm
1 Human beings	Death, disease, serious injury, genetic mutation, birth defects or the impairment of reproductive functions. For these purposes, disease is to be taken to mean an unhealthy condition of the body or a part of it and can include, for example, cancer, liver dysfunction or extensive skin ailments. Mental dysfunction is included only insofar as it is attributable to the effects of a pollutant on the body of the person concerned. In this Chapter, this description of significant harm is referred to as a 'human health effect'.
2 Any ecological system, or living organism forming part of such a system, within a location which is: ● an area notified as an area of special scientific interest under section 28 of the Wildlife and Countryside Act 1981; ● any land declared a national nature reserve under section 35 of that Act; ● any area designated as a marine nature reserve under section 36 of that Act; ● an area of special protection for birds, established under section 3 of that Act; ● any European Site within the meaning of regulation 10 of the Conservation (Natural Habitats etc.) Regulations 1994 (i.e., Special Areas of Conservation and Special Protection Areas); ● any candidate Special Areas of Conservation or potential Special Protection Areas given equivalent protection; ● any habitat or site afforded policy protection under paragraph 13 of Planning Policy Guidance Note 9 (PPG9) on nature conservation (i.e., candidate Special Areas of Conservation, potential Special Protection Areas and listed Ramsar sites); or ● any nature reserve established under section 21 of the National Parks and Access to the Countryside Act 1949.	For *any* protected location: ● harm which results in an irreversible adverse change, or in some other substantial adverse change, in the functioning of the ecological system within any substantial part of that location; or ● harm which affects any species of special interest within that location and which endangers the long-term maintenance of the population of that species at that location. In addition, in the case of a protected location which is a European Site (or a candidate Special Area of Conservation or a potential Special Protection Area), harm which is incompatible with the favourable conservation status of natural habitats at that location or species typically found there. In determining what constitutes such harm, the local authority should have regard to the advice of English Nature and to the requirements of the Conservation (Natural Habitats etc.) Regulations 1994. In this Chapter, this description of significant harm is referred to as an 'ecological system effect'.
3 Property in the form of: ● crops, including timber; ● produce grown domestically, or on allotments, for consumption; ● livestock; ● other owned or domesticated animals; ● wild animals which are the subject of shooting or fishing rights.	For crops, a substantial diminution in yield or other substantial loss in their value resulting from death, disease or other physical damage. For domestic pets, death, serious disease or serious physical damage. For other property in this category, a substantial loss in its value resulting from death, disease or other serious physical damage. The local authority should regard a substantial loss in value as occurring only when a substantial proportion of the animals or crops are dead or otherwise no longer fit for their intended purposes. Food should be regarded as being no longer fit for purpose when it fails to comply with the provisions of the Food Safety Act 1990. Where a diminution in yield or loss in value is caused by a pollutant linkage, a 20% diminution or loss should be regarded as a benchmark for what constitutes a substantial diminution or loss. In this Chapter, this description of significant harm is referred to as an 'animal or crop effect'.

Type of Receptor	Description of harm to that type of receptor that is to be regarded as significant harm
4 Property in the form of buildings. For this purpose, 'building' means any structure or erection, and any part of a building including any part below ground level, but does not include plant or machinery comprised in a building.	Structural failure, substantial damage or substantial interference with any right of occupation. For this purpose, the local authority should regard substantial damage or substantial interference as occurring when any part of the building ceases to be capable of being used for the purpose for which it is or was intended. Additionally, in the case of a scheduled Ancient Monument, substantial damage should be regarded as occurring when the damage significantly impairs the historic, architectural, traditional, artistic or archaeological interest by reason of which the monument was scheduled. In this chapter, this description of significant harm is referred to as a 'building effect'.

WHETHER THE POSSIBILITY OF SIGNIFICANT HARM BEING CAUSED IS SIGNIFICANT

A.27   As stated in paragraph A.9 above, the guidance on determining whether a particular possibility is significant is based on the principles of risk assessment, and in particular on considerations of the magnitude or consequences of the different types of significant harm caused. The term 'possibility of significant harm being caused' should be taken as referring to a measure of the probability, or frequency, of the occurrence of circumstances which would lead to significant harm being caused.

A.28   The local authority should take into account the following factors in deciding whether the possibility of significant harm being caused is significant:

(a)   the nature and degree of harm;

(b)   the susceptibility of the receptors to which the harm might be caused; and

(c)   the timescale within which the harm might occur.

A.29   In considering the timescale, the authority should take into account any evidence that the current use of the land (as defined in paragraphs A.25 and A.26 above) will cease in the foreseeable future.

A.30   The local authority should regard as a significant possibility any possibility of significant harm which meets the conditions set out in Table B for the description of significant harm under consideration.

A.31   In Table B, references to 'relevant information' mean information which is:

(a)   scientifically-based;

(b)   authoritative;

(c)   relevant to the assessment of risks arising from the presence of contaminants in soil; and

(d)   appropriate to the determination of whether any land is contaminated land for the purposes of Part IIA, in that the use of the information is consistent with providing a level of protection of risk in line with the qualitative criteria set out in Tables A and B.

A.32   In general, when considering significant harm to non-human receptors, the local authority should apply the tests set out in the relevant entries in Table B to determine whether there is a significant possibility of that harm being caused.

However, the local authority may also determine that there is a significant possibility of significant harm with respect to a non-human receptor in any case where the conditions in the third, fourth and fifth entries in Table B are not met, but where:

(a) there is a reasonable possibility of significant harm being caused; and

(b) that harm would result from either:

(i) a single incident such as a fire or explosion, or

(ii) a short-term (that is, less than 24-hour) exposure of the receptor to the pollutant.

Table B — Significant Possibility of Significant Harm

Descriptions Of Significant Harm (As Defined in Table A)	Conditions For There Being a Significant Possibility Of Significant Harm
1 Human health effects arising from: • the intake of a contaminant, or • other direct bodily contact with a contaminant.	If the amount of the pollutant in the pollutant linkage in question: • which a human receptor in that linkage might take in, or • to which such a human might otherwise be exposed, as a result of the pathway in that linkage, would represent an unacceptable intake or direct bodily contact, assessed on the basis of relevant information on the toxicological properties of that pollutant. Such an assessment should take into account: • the likely total intake of, or exposure to, the substance or substances which form the pollutant, from all sources including that from the pollutant linkage in question; • the relative contribution of the pollutant linkage in question to the likely aggregate intake of, or exposure to, the relevant substance or substances; and • the duration of intake or exposure resulting from the pollutant linkage in question. The question of whether an intake or exposure is unacceptable is independent of the number of people who might experience or be affected by that intake or exposure. Toxicological properties should be taken to include carcinogenic, mutagenic, teratogenic, pathogenic, endocrine-disrupting and other similar properties.
2 All other human health effects (particularly by way of explosion or fire).	If the probability, or frequency, of occurrence of significant harm of that description is unacceptable, assessed on the basis of relevant information concerning: • that type of pollutant linkage, or • that type of significant harm arising from other causes. In making such an assessment, the local authority should take into account the levels of risk which have been judged unacceptable in other similar contexts and should give particular weight to cases where the pollutant linkage might cause significant harm which: • would be irreversible or incapable of being treated; • would affect a substantial number of people; • would result from a single incident such as a fire or an explosion; or • would be likely to result from a short-term (that is, less than 24-hour) exposure to the pollutant.
3 All ecological system effects.	If either: • significant harm of that description is more likely than not to result from the pollutant linkage in question; or • there is a reasonable possibility of significant harm of that description being caused, and if that harm were to occur, it would result in such a degree of damage to features of special interest at the location in question that they would be beyond any practicable possibility of restoration. Any assessment made for these purposes should take into account relevant information for that type of pollutant linkage, particularly in relation to the ecotoxicological effects of the pollutant
4 All animal and crop effects.	If significant harm of that description is more likely than not to result from the pollutant linkage in question, taking into account relevant information for that type of pollutant linkage, particularly in relation to the ecotoxicological effects of the pollutant.

Descriptions Of Significant Harm (As Defined in Table A)	Conditions For There Being a Significant Possibility Of Significant Harm
5 All building effects.	If significant harm of that description is more likely than not to result from the pollutant linkage in question during the expected economic life of the building (or, in the case of a scheduled Ancient Monument, the foreseeable future), taking into account relevant information for that type of pollutant linkage.

A.33   The possibility of significant harm being caused as a result of any change of use of any land to one which is not a current use of that land (as defined in paragraph A.26 above) should not be regarded as a significant possibility for the purposes of this Chapter.

A.34   When considering the possibility of significant harm being caused in relation to any future use or development which falls within the description of a 'current use' as a result of paragraph A.26(b) above, the local authority should assume that if the future use is introduced, or the development carried out, this will be done in accordance with any existing planning permission for that use or development. In particular, the local authority should assume:

(a)   that any remediation which is the subject of a condition attached to that planning permission, or is the subject of any planning obligation, will be carried out in accordance with that permission or obligation; and

(b)   where a planning permission has been given subject to conditions which require steps to be taken to prevent problems which might be caused by contamination, and those steps are to be approved by the local planning authority, that the local planning authority will ensure that those steps include adequate remediation.

PART 4   THE POLLUTION OF CONTROLLED WATERS

A.35   Section 78A(9) defines the pollution of controlled waters as:
'the entry into controlled waters of any poisonous, noxious or polluting matter or any solid waste matter'.

A.36   Before determining that pollution of controlled waters is being, or is likely to be, caused, the local authority should be satisfied that a substance is continuing to enter controlled waters or is likely to enter controlled waters. For this purpose, the local authority should regard something as being 'likely' when they judge it more likely than not to occur.

A.37   Land should not be designated as contaminated land where:

(a)   a substance is already present in controlled waters;

(b)   entry into controlled waters of that substance from land has ceased; and

(c)   it is not likely that further entry will take place.

A.38   Substances should be regarded as having entered controlled waters where:

(a)   they are dissolved or suspended in those waters; or

(b)   if they are immiscible with water, they have direct contact with those waters on or beneath the surface of the water.

A.39   The term 'continuing to enter' should be taken to mean any entry additional to any which has already occurred.

CHAPTER B   STATUTORY GUIDANCE ON THE IDENTIFICATION OF CONTAMINATED LAND

PART 1   SCOPE OF THE CHAPTER

B.1   The statutory guidance in this Chapter is issued under sections 78A(2) and 78B(2) of Part IIA of the Environmental Protection Act 1990, and provides guidance on the inspection of its area by a local authority and the manner in which an authority is to determine whether any land appears to it to be contaminated land.

B.2   Section 78B(1) provides that:
'Every local authority shall cause its area to be inspected from time to time for the purpose—
(a)   of identifying contaminated land; and
(b)   of enabling the authority to decide whether any such land is land which is required to be designated as a special site.'

B.3   Section 78B(2) further provides that:
'In performing [these] functions . . . a local authority shall act in accordance with any guidance issued for the purpose by the Secretary of State.'

B.4   Section 78A(2) also provides that:
' "Contaminated land" is any land which appears to the local authority in whose area it is situated to be in such a condition, by reason of substances in, on or under the land, that—
(a)   significant harm is being caused or there is a significant possibility of such harm being caused, or
(b)   pollution of controlled waters is being, or is likely to be, caused;
and, in determining whether any land appears to be such land, a local authority shall, . . . act in accordance with guidance issued by the Secretary of State . . . with respect to the manner in which that determination is to be made.'

B.5   The local authority is therefore required to act in accordance with the statutory guidance contained in this Chapter.

B.6   The questions of what harm is to be regarded as significant, whether the possibility of significant harm being caused is significant, and whether pollution of controlled waters is being or is likely to be caused are to be determined in accordance with guidance contained in Chapter A.

PART 2   DEFINITIONS OF TERMS

B.7   Unless otherwise stated, any word, term or phrase given a specific meaning in Part IIA of the Environmental Protection Act 1990, or in the guidance at Chapter A, has the same meaning for the purposes of the guidance in this Chapter.

B.8   Any reference to 'Part IIA' means 'Part IIA of the Environmental Protection Act 1990'. Any reference to a 'section' in primary legislation means a section of the Environmental Protection Act 1990, unless it is specifically stated otherwise.

PART 3 THE LOCAL AUTHORITY'S INSPECTION DUTY

STRATEGIC APPROACH TO INSPECTION

B.9 In carrying out its inspection duty under section 78B(1), the local authority should take a strategic approach to the identification of land which merits detailed individual inspection. This approach should:

(a) be rational, ordered and efficient;

(b) be proportionate to the seriousness of any actual or potential risk;

(c) seek to ensure that the most pressing and serious problems are located first;

(d) ensure that resources are concentrated on investigating in areas where the authority is most likely to identify contaminated land; and

(c) ensure that the local authority efficiently identifies requirements for the detailed inspection of particular areas of land.

B.10 In developing this strategic approach the local authority should reflect local circumstances. In particular it should consider:

(a) any available evidence that significant harm or pollution of controlled waters is actually being caused;

(b) the extent to which any receptor (which is either of a type listed in Table A in Chapter A or is controlled waters) is likely to be found in any of the different parts of the authority's area;

(c) the extent to which any of those receptors is likely to be exposed to a contaminant (as defined in Chapter A), for example as a result of the use of the land or of the geological and hydrogeological features of the area;

(d) the extent to which information on land contamination is already available;

(c) the history, scale and nature of industrial or other activities which may have contaminated the land in different parts of its area;

(f) the nature and timing of past redevelopment in different parts of its area;

(g) the extent to which remedial action has already been taken by the authority or others to deal with land-contamination problems or is likely to be taken as part of an impending redevelopment; and

(h) the extent to which other regulatory authorities are likely to be considering the possibility of harm being caused to particular receptors or the likelihood of any pollution of controlled waters being caused in particular parts of the local authority's area.

B.11 In developing its strategic approach, the local authority should consult the Environment Agency and other appropriate public authorities, such as the county council (where one exists), statutory regeneration bodies, English Nature, English Heritage and the Ministry of Agriculture, Fisheries and Food.

B.12 The local authority should set out its approach as a written strategy, which it should formally adopt and publish. This strategy should be published within 15 months of the issue of this guidance. As soon as its strategy is published, the local authority should send a copy to the Environment Agency.

B.13 The local authority should keep its strategy under periodic review.

B.14   The local authority should not await the publication of its strategy before commencing more detailed work investigating particular areas of land, where this appears necessary.

CONTENTS OF THE STRATEGY

B.15   Strategies are likely to vary both between to local authorities and between different parts of an authority's area, reflecting the different problems associated with land contamination in different areas. The local authority should include in its strategy:

(a)   a description of the particular characteristics of its area and how that influences its approach;

(h)   the authority's particular aims, objectives and priorities;

(c)   appropriate timescales for the inspection of different parts of its area; and

(d)   arrangements and procedures for:

(i)   considering land for which it may itself have responsibilities by virtue of its current or former ownership or occupation,

(ii)   obtaining and evaluating information on actual harm, or pollution of controlled waters,

(iii)   identifying receptors, and assessing the possibility or likelihood that they are being, or could be, exposed to or affected by a contaminant,

(iv)   obtaining and evaluating existing information on the possible presence of contaminants and their effects,

(v)   liaison with, and responding to information from, other statutory bodies, including, in particular, the Environment Agency, English Nature and the Ministry of Agriculture, Fisheries and Food (see paragraphs B.16 and B.17 below),

(vi)   liaison with, and responding to information from, the owners or occupiers of land, and other relevant interested parties,

(vii)   responding to information or complaints from members of the public, businesses and voluntary organisations,

(viii)   planning and reviewing a programme for inspecting particular areas of land,

(ix)   carrying out the detailed inspection of particular areas of land,

(x)   reviewing and updating assumptions and information previously used to assess the need for detailed inspection of different areas, and managing new information, and

(xi)   managing information obtained and held in the course of carrying out its inspection duties.

INFORMATION FROM OTHER STATUTORY BODIES

B.16   Other regulatory authorities may be able to provide information relevant to the identification of land as contaminated land, as a result of their various complementary functions. The local authority should seek to make specific arrangements with such other bodies to avoid unnecessary duplication in investigation.

B.17   For example, the Environment Agency has general responsibilities for the protection of the water environment. It monitors the quality of controlled waters and in doing so may discover land which would appropriately be identified as contaminated land by reason of pollution of controlled waters which is being, or is likely to be, caused.

INSPECTING PARTICULAR AREAS OF LAND

B.18   Applying the strategy will result in the identification of particular areas of land where it is possible that a pollutant linkage exists. Subject to the guidance in paragraphs B.22 to B.25 and B.27 to B.30 below, the local authority should carry out a detailed inspection of any such area to obtain sufficient information for the authority.

(a)   to determine, in accordance with the guidance on the manner of determination in Part 4 below, whether that land appears to be contaminated land; and

(b)   to decide whether any such land falls within the definition of a special site prescribed in regulations 2 and 3 of the Contaminated Land (England) Regulations 2000, and is therefore required to be designated as a special site.

B.19   To be sufficient for the first of these purposes the information should include, in particular, evidence of the actual presence of a pollutant.

B.20   Detailed inspection may include any or all of the following:

(a)   the collation and assessment of documentary information, or other information from other bodies;

(b)   a visit to the particular area for the purposes of visual inspection and, in some cases, limited sampling (for example of surface deposits); or

(c)   intrusive investigation of the land (for example by exploratory excavations).

B.21   Section 108 of the Environment Act 1995 gives the local authority the power to authorise a person to exercise specific powers of entry. For the purposes of this Chapter, any detailed inspection of land carried out through use of this power by the local authority is referred to as an 'inspection using statutory powers of entry'.

B.22   Before the local authority carries out an inspection using statutory powers of entry, it should be satisfied, on the basis of any information already obtained:

(a)   in all cases, that there is a reasonable possibility that a pollutant linkage (as defined in Chapter A) exists on the land; this implies that not only must the authority be satisfied that there is a reasonable possibility of the presence of a contaminant, a receptor and a pathway, but also that these would together create a pollutant linkage; and

(b)   further, in cases involving an intrusive investigation,

(i)   that it is likely that the contaminant is actually present, and

(ii)   given the current use of the land as defined at paragraph A.26, that the receptor is actually present or is likely to be present.

B.23   The local authority should not carry out any inspection using statutory powers of entry which takes the form of intrusive investigation if:

(a)   it has already been provided with detailed information on the condition of the land, whether by the Environment Agency or some other person such as the owner of the land, which provides an appropriate basis upon which the local authority can determine whether the land is contaminated land in accordance with the requirements of the guidance in this Chapter; or

(b)   a person offers to provide such information within a reasonable and specified time, and then provides such information within that time.

B.24   The local authority should carry out any intrusive investigation in accordance with appropriate technical procedures for such investigations. It should also ensure that it takes all reasonable precautions to avoid harm, water pollution or damage to natural resources or features of historical or archaeological interest which might be caused as a result of its investigation. Before carrying out any intrusive investigation on any area notified as an area of special scientific interest (SSSI), the local authority should consult English Nature on any action which, if carried out by the owner or occupier, would require the consent of English Nature under section 28 of the Wildlife and Countryside Act 1981.

B.25   If at any stage, the local authority considers, on the basis of information obtained from a detailed inspection, that there is no longer a reasonable possibility that a particular pollutant linkage exists on the land, the authority should not carry out any further detailed inspection for that pollutant linkage.

LAND WHICH MAY BE A SPECIAL SITE

B.26   If land has been determined to be contaminated land and it also falls within one or more of the 'special sites' descriptions prescribed in regulations made under Part IIA, it is required to be designated as a special site. The Environment Agency then becomes the enforcing authority for that land. It is therefore helpful for the Environment Agency to have a formal role at the inspection stage for any such land.

B.27   Before authorising or carrying out on any land an inspection using statutory powers of entry, the local authority should consider whether, if that land were found to be contaminated land, it would meet any of the descriptions of land prescribed in the Regulations as requiring to be designated a special site.

B.28   If the local authority already has information that this would be the case, the authority should always seek to make arrangements with the Environment Agency for that Agency to carry out the inspection of the land on behalf of the local authority. This might occur, for example, where the prescribed description of land in the Regulations relates to its current or former use, such as land on which a process designated for central control under the Integrated Pollution Control regime has been carried out, or land which is occupied by the Ministry of Defence.

B.29   If the local authority considers that there is a reasonable possibility that a particular pollutant linkage is present, and the presence of a linkage of that kind would require the designation of the land as a special site (were that linkage found to be a significant pollutant linkage), the authority should seek to make arrangements with the Environment Agency for the Agency to carry out the inspection of the land. An example of this kind of pollutant linkage would be the pollution of waters in the circumstances described in regulation 3(b) of the Contaminated Land (England) Regulations 2000.

B.30　Where the Environment Agency is to carry out an inspection on behalf of the local authority, the authority should, where necessary, authorise a person nominated by the Agency to exercise the powers of entry conferred by section 108 of the Environment Act 1995. Before the local authority gives such an authorisation, the Environment Agency should satisfy the local authority that the conditions for the use of the statutory powers of entry set out in paragraphs B.22 to B.25 above are met.

PART 4　DETERMINING WHETHER LAND APPEARS TO BE CONTAMINATED LAND

B.31　The local authority has the sole responsibility for determining whether any land appears to be contaminated land. It cannot delegate this responsibility (except in accordance with section 101 of the Local Government Act 1972), although in discharging it the local authority can choose to rely on information or advice provided by another body such as the Environment Agency, or by a consultant appointed for that purpose. This applies even where the Agency has carried out the inspection of land on behalf of the local authority (see paragraphs B.26 to B.30 above).

PHYSICAL EXTENT OF LAND

B.32　A determination that land is contaminated land is necessarily made in respect of a specific area of land. In deciding what that area should be, the primary consideration is the extent of the land which is contaminated land. However, there may be situations in which the local authority may consider that separate designations of parts of a larger area of contaminated land may simplify the administration of the consequential actions. In such circumstances, the local authority should do so, taking into account:

(a)　the location of significant pollutants in, on or under the land;

(b)　the nature of the remediation which might be required; and

(c)　the likely identity of those who may be the appropriate persons to bear responsibility for the remediation (where this is reasonably clear at this stage).

B.33　If necessary, the local authority should initially review a wider area, the history of which suggests that contamination problems are likely. It can subsequently refine this down to the precise areas which meet the statutory tests for identification as contaminated land, and use these as the basis for its determination.

B.34　In practice, the land to be covered by a single determination is likely to be the smallest area which is covered by a single remediation action which cannot sensibly be broken down into smaller actions. Subject to this, the land is likely to be the smaller of:

(a)　the plots which are separately recorded in the Land Register or are in separate ownership or occupation; and

(b)　the area of land in which the presence of significant pollutants has been established.

B.35   The determination should identify the area of contaminated land clearly, including reference to a map or plan at an appropriate scale.

B.36   The local authority should also be prepared to review the decision on the physical extent of the land to be identified in the light of further information.

MAKING THE DETERMINATION

B.37   In determining whether any land appears to the local authority to be contaminated land, the authority is required to act in accordance with the guidance on the definition of contaminated land set out in Chapter A. Guidance on the manner in which the local authority should determine whether land appears to it to be contaminated land, by reason of substances in, on or under the land, is set out in paragraphs B.39 to B.51 below.

B.38   There are four possible grounds for the determination (corresponding to the parts of the definition of contaminated land in section 78A(2)) namely that:

(a)   significant harm is being caused (see paragraph B.44 below);

(b)   there is a significant possibility of significant harm being caused (see paragraphs B.45 to B.49 below);

(c)   pollution of controlled waters is being caused (see paragraph B.50 below); or

(d)   pollution of controlled waters is likely to be caused (see paragraph B.51 below).

B.39   In making any determination, the local authority should take all relevant and available evidence into account and carry out an appropriate scientific and technical assessment of that evidence.

B.40   The local authority should identify a particular polltitant linkage or linkages (as defined in Chapter A) as the basis for the determination. All three elements of any pollutant linkage (pollutant, pathway and receptor) should be identified. A linkage which forms a basis for the determination that land is contaminated land is then a 'significant pollutant linkage'; and any pollutant which forms part of it is a 'significant pollutant'.

B.41   The local authority should consider whether:

(a)   there is evidence that additive or synergistic effects between potential pollutants, whether between the same substance on different areas of land or between different substances, may result in a significant pollutant linkage;

(b)   a combination of several different potential pathways linking one or more potential pollutants to a particular receptor, or to a particular class of receptors, may result in a significant pollutant linkage; and

(c)   there is more than one significant pollutant linkage on any land; if there are, each should be considered separately, since different people may be responsible for the remediation.

Consistency with Other Statutory Bodies

B.42   In making a determination which relates to an 'ecological system effect' as defined in Table A of Chapter A, the local authority should adopt an approach consistent with that adopted by English Nature. To this end, the local authority should consult that authority and have regard to its comments in making its determination.

B.43   In making a determination which relates to pollution of controlled waters the local authority should adopt an approach consistent with that adopted by the Environment Agency in applying relevant statutory provisions. To this end, where the local authority is considering whether pollution of controlled waters is being or is likely to be caused, it should consult the Environment Agency and have regard to its comments before determining whether pollution of controlled waters is being or is likely to be caused.

Determining that 'Significant Harm is being Caused'

B.44   The local authority should determine that land is contaminated land on the basis that significant harm is being caused where:

(a)   it has carried out an appropriate scientific and technical assessment of all the relevant and available evidence; and

(b)   on the basis of that assessment, it is satisfied on the balance of probabilities that significant harm is being caused.

Determining that 'There is a Significant Possibility of Significant Harm being Caused

B.45   The local authority should determine that land is contaminated land on the basis that there is a significant possibility of significant harm being caused (as defined in Chapter A), where:

(a)   it has carried out a scientific and technical assessment of the risks arising from the pollutant linkage, according to relevant, appropriate, authoritative and scientifically based guidance on such risk assessments;

(b)   that assessment shows that there is a significant possibility of significant harm being caused; and

(c)   there are no suitable and sufficient risk management arrangements in place to prevent such harm.

B.46   In following any such guidance on risk assessment, the local authority should be satisfied that it is relevant to the circumstances of the pollutant linkage and land in question, and that any appropriate allowances have been made for particular circumstances.

B.47   To simplify such in assessment of risks, the local authority may use authoritative and scientifically based guideline values for concentrations of the potential pollutants in, on or under the land in pollutant linkages of the type concerned. If it does so, the local authority should be satisfied that:

(a)   an adequate scientific and technical assessment of the information on the potential pollutant, using the appropriate, authoritative and scientifically based guideline values, shows that there is a significant possibility of significant harm; and

(b)   there are no suitable and sufficient risk management arrangements in place to prevent such harm.

B.48   In using any guideline values, the local authority should be satisfied that:

(a)   the guideline values are relevant to the judgement of whether the effects of the pollutant linkage in question constitute a significant possibility of significant harm;

(b)   the assumptions underlying the derivation of any numerical values in the guideline values (for example, assumptions regarding soil conditions, the behaviour of potential pollutants, the existence of pathways, the land-use patterns, and the availability of receptors) are relevant to the circumstances of the pollutant linkage in question;

(c)   any other conditions relevant to the use of the guideline values have been observed (for example, the number of samples taken or the methods of preparation and analysis of those samples); and

(d)   appropriate adjustments have been made to allow for the differences between the circumstances of the land in question and any assumptions or other factors relating to the guideline values.

B.49   The local authority should be prepared to reconsider any determination based on such use of guideline values if it is demonstrated to the authority's satisfaction that under some other more appropriate method of assessing the risks the local authority would not have determined that the land appeared to be contaminated land.

Determining that 'Pollution of Controlled Waters is being Caused

B.50   The local authority should determine that land is contaminated land on the basis that pollution of controlled waters is being caused where:

(a)   it has carried out an appropriate scientific and technical assessment of all the relevant and available evidence, having regard to any advice provided by the Environment Agency; and

(b)   on the basis of that assessment, it is satisfied on the balance of probabilities that both of the following circumstances apply:

(i)   a potential pollutant is present in, on or under the land in question, which constitutes poisonous, noxious or polluting matter, or which is solid waste matter, and

(ii)   that potential pollutant is entering controlled waters by the pathway identified in the pollutant linkage,

Determining that 'Pollution of Controlled Waters is Likely to be Caused'

B.51   The local authority should determine that land is contaminated land on the basis that pollution of controlled waters is likely to be caused where:

(a)   it has carried out an appropriate scientific and technical assessment of all the relevant and available evidence, having regard to any advice provided by the Environment Agency; and

(b)   on the basis of that assessment it is satisfied that, on the balance of probabilities, all of the following circumstances apply:

(i)   a potential pollutant is present in, on or under the land in question, which constitutes poisonous, noxious or polluting matter, or which is solid waste matter,

(ii)   the potential pollutant in question is in such a condition that it is capable of entering controlled waters,

(iii)   taking into account the geology and other circumstances of the land in question, there is a pathway (as defined in Chapter A) by which the potential pollutant can enter identified controlled waters,

(iv)   the potential pollutant in question is more likely than not to enter these controlled waters and, when it enters the controlled waters, will be in a form that is poisonous, noxious or polluting, or solid waste matter, and

(v)   there are no suitable and sufficient risk management arrangements relevant to the pollution linkage in place to prevent such pollution.

RECORD OF THE DETERMINATION THAT LAND IS CONTAMINATED LAND

B.52   The local authority should prepare a written record of any determination that particular land is contaminated land. The record should include (by means of a reference to other documents if necessary):

(a)   a description of the particular significant pollutant linkage, identifying all three components of pollutant, pathway and receptor;

(b)   a summary of the evidence upon which the determination is based;

(c)   a summary of the relevant assessment of this evidence; and

(d)   a summary of the way in which the authority considers that the requirements of the guidance in this Part and in Chapter A of the guidance have been satisfied.

CHAPTER C   STATUTORY GUIDANCE ON THE REMEDIATION OF CONTAMINATED LAND

PART 1   SCOPE OF THE CHAPTER

C.1   The statutory guidance in this Chapter is issued under section 78E(5) of Part IIA of the Environmental Protection Act 1990, and provides guidance on the remediation which may be required for any contaminated land.

C.2   Section 78E provides:

'(4)   The only things by way of remediation which the enforcing authority may do, or require to be done, under or by virtue of [Part IIA of the Environmental Protection Act 1990] are things which it considers reasonable, having regard to—

(a)   the cost which is likely to be involved; and

(b)   the seriousness of the harm, or pollution of controlled waters, in question.

(5)   In determining for any purpose of this Part—

(a)   what is to be done (whether by an appropriate person, the enforcing authority, or any other person) by way of remediation in any particular case,

(b)   the standard to which any land is, or waters are, to be remediated pursuant to [a remediation] notice, or

(c)   what is, or is not, to be regarded as reasonable for the purposes of subsection (4) above,
the enforcing authority shall have regard to any guidance issued for the purpose by the Secretary of State'.

C.3   The enforcing authority is therefore required to have regard to this guidance when it is:

(a)   determining what remediation action it should specify in a remediation notice as being required to be carried out (section 78E(1));

(b)   satisfying itself that appropriate remediation is being, or will be, carried out without the service of a notice (section 78H(s)(b)); or

(c)   deciding what remediation action it should carry out itself (section 78N).

C.4   The guidance in this Chapter does not attempt to set out detailed technical procedures or working methods. For information on these matters, the enforcing authority may wish to consult relevant technical documents prepared under the contaminated land research programmes of DETR and the Environment Agency, and by other professional and technical organisations.

PART 2   DEFINITIONS OF TERMS

C.5   Unless otherwise stated, any word, term or phrase given a specific meaning in Part IIA of the Environmental Protection Act 1990, or in the statutory guidance in Chapters A or B, has the same meaning for the purposes of the guidance in this Chapter.

C.6   'Remediation' is defined in section 78A(7) as meaning:

(a)   the doing of anything for the purpose of assessing the condition of—

(i)   the contaminated land in question;

(ii)   any controlled waters affected by that land; or

(iii)   any land adjoining or adjacent to that land;

(b)   the doing of any works, the carrying out of any operations or the taking of any steps in relation to any such land or waters for the purpose—

(i)   of preventing or minimising, or remedying or mitigating the effects of, any significant harm, or any pollution of controlled waters, by reason of which the contaminated land is such land; or

(ii)   of restoring the land or waters to their former state; or

(c)   the making of subsequent inspections from time to time for the purpose of keeping under review the condition of the land or waters.'

C.7   The definition of remediation given in section 78A extends more widely than the common usage of the term, which more normally relates only to the actions defined as 'remedial treatment actions' below.

C.8   For the purposes of the guidance in this Chapter, the following definitions apply:

(a)   a 'remediation action' is any individual thing which is being, or is to be, done by way of remediation;

(b)   a 'remediation package' is the full set or sequence of remediation actions, within a remediation scheme, which are referable to a particular significant pollutant linkage;

(c)   a 'remediation scheme' is the complete set or sequence of remediation actions (referable to one or more significant pollutant linkages) to be carried out with respect to the relevant land or waters;

(d)   'relevant land or waters' means the contaminated land in question, any controlled waters affected by that land and any land adjoining or adjacent to the contaminated land on which remediation might be required as a consequence of the contaminated land being such land;

(c)   an 'assessment action' means a remediation action falling within the definition of remediation in section 78A(7) (a) (see paragraph C.6 above);

(f)   a 'remedial treatment action' means a remediation action falling within the definition in section 78A(7)(b) (see paragraph C.6 above); and

(g)   a 'monitoring action' means a remediation action falling within the definition in section 78A(7)(c) (see paragraph C.6 above).

C.9   Any reference to 'Part IIA' means 'Part IIA of the Environmental Protection Act 1990'. Any reference to a 'section' in primary legislation means a section of the Environmental Protection Act 1990, unless it is specifically stated otherwise.

PART 3   SECURING REMEDIATION

C.10   When the enforcing authority is serving a remediation notice, it will need to specify in that notice any remediation action which is needed in order to achieve remediation of the relevant land or waters to the standard described in Part 4 of this Chapter and which is reasonable for the purposes of section 78E(4) (see Part 5 of this Chapter). Part 6 of this Chapter provides further guidance relevant to determining the necessary standard of remediation. Part 7 provides guidance on the circumstances in which different types of remediation action may, or may not, be required.

C.11   The enforcing authority should be satisfied that appropriate remediation is being, or will be, carried out without the service of a remediation notice if that remediation would remediate the relevant land or waters to an equivalent, or better, standard than would be achieved by the remediation action or actions that the authority could, at that time, otherwise specify in a remediation notice.

PHASED REMEDIATION

C.12   The overall process of remediation on any land or waters may require a phased approach, with different remediation actions being carried out in sequence. For example, the local authority may have obtained sufficient information about the relevant land or waters to enable it to identify the land as falling within the definition of contaminated land, but that information may not be sufficient information for the enforcing authority to be able to specify any particular remedial treatment action as being appropriate. Further assessment actions may be needed in any case of this kind as part of the remediation scheme. In other cases, successive phases of remedial treatment actions may be needed.

C.13   The phasing of remediation is likely to follow a progression from assessment actions, through remedial treatment actions and onto monitoring actions. However, this will not always be the case, and the phasing may omit some stages or revisit others. For example, in some circumstances it may be possible for a remedial treatment action to be carried out without any previous assessment action (because sufficient information is already available). But, conversely, in some instances additional assessment action may be found to be necessary only in the light of information derived during the course of a first phase of a required assessment action or the carrying out of required remedial treatment actions.

C.14   Where it is necessary for the remediation scheme as a whole to be phased, a single remediation notice may not be able to include all of the remediation actions which could eventually be needed. In these circumstances, the enforcing authority should specify in the notice the remediation action or actions which, on the basis of the information available at that time, it considers to be appropriate, taking into account in particular the guidance in Part 7 of this Chapter. In due course, the authority may need to serve further remediation notices which include remediation actions for further phases of the scheme.

C.15   However before serving any further remediation notice, the enforcing authority must be satisfied that the contaminated land which was originally identified still appears to it to meet the definition in section 78A(2). If, for example, the information obtained as a result of an assessment action reveals that there is not, in fact, a significant possibility of significant harm being caused, nor is there a likelihood of any pollution of controlled waters being caused, then no further assessment, remedial treatment or monitoring action can be required under section 78E(1).

PART 4   THE STANDARD TO WHICH LAND OR WATERS SHOULD BE REMEDIATED

C.16   The statutory guidance in this Part is issued under section 78E(5)(b) and provides guidance on the standard to which land or waters should be remediated.

THE STANDARD OF REMEDIATION

C.17   The Government's intention is that any remediation required under this regime should result in land being 'suitable for use'. The aim of any remediation should be to ensure that the circumstances of the land are such that, in its current use (as defined in paragraph A.26 of Chapter A) it is no longer contaminated land (as defined in section 78A(2)), and that the effects of any significant harm or pollution of controlled waters which has occurred are remedied. However, it is always open to the appropriate person to carry out remediation on a broader basis than this, if he considers it in his interests to do so, for example if he wishes to prepare the land for redevelopment.

C.18   The standard to which the relevant land or waters as a whole should be remediated should be established by considering separately each significant pollutant linkage identified on the land in question. For each such linkage, the standard of remediation should be that which would be achieved by the use of a remediation package which forms the best practicable techniques of remediation for:

(a)   ensuring that the linkage is no longer a significant pollutant linkage, by doing any one or more of the following:

  (i) removing or treating the pollutant;

  (ii) breaking or removing the pathway; or

  (iii) protecting or removing the receptor; and

 (b) remedying the effect of any significant harm or pollution of controlled waters which is resulting, or has already resulted from, the significant pollutant linkage.

 C.19 In deciding what represents the best practicable technique for any particular remediation, the enforcing authority should look for the method of achieving the desired results which, in the light of the nature and volume of the significant pollutant concerned and the timescale within which remediation is required:

 (a) is reasonable, taking account of the guidance in Part 5; and

 (b) represents the best combination of the following qualities:

  (i) practicability, both in general and in the particular circumstances of the relevant land or waters;

  (ii) effectiveness in achieving the aims set out in paragraph C. 18 above; and

  (iii) durability in maintaining that effectiveness over the timescale within which the significant harm or pollution of controlled waters may occur.

 C.20 Further guidance on how the factors set out in sub-paragraph (b) above should be considered is set out in Part 6. The determination of what, in any particular case, represents the best practicable technique of remediation may require a balance to be struck between these factors.

 C.21 When considering what would be the best practicable techniques for remediation in any particular case, the enforcing authority should work on the basis of authoritative scientific and technical advice. The authority should consider what comparable techniques have recently been carried out successfully on other land, and also any technological advances and changes in scientific knowledge and understanding.

 C.22 Where there is established good practice for the remediation of a particular type of significant pollutant linkage, the authority should assume that this represents the best practicable technique for remediation for a linkage of that type, provided that:

 (a) it is satisfied that the use of that means of remediation is appropriate, given the circumstances of the relevant land or waters; and

 (b) the remediation actions involved would be reasonable having regard to the cost which is likely to be involved and the seriousness of the harm or pollution of controlled waters in question.

 C.23 In some instances, the best practicable techniques of remediation with respect to any significant pollutant linkage may not fully achieve the aim in subparagraph C.18(a), that is to say that if the remediation were to be carried out the pollutant linkage in question would remain a significant pollutant linkage. Where this applies, the standard of remediation with respect to that significant pollutant linkage should be that which, by the use of the best practicable techniques:

 (a) comes as close as practicable to achieving the aim in subparagraph C. 18(a);

(b)   achieves the aim in subparagraph C.18(b); and

(c)   puts arrangements in place to remedy the effect of any significant harm or pollution of controlled waters which may be caused in the future as a consequence of the continued existence of the pollutant linkage.

C.24   In addition, the best practicable techniques for remediation with respect to a significant pollutant linkage may, in some circumstances, not fully remedy the effect of past or future significant harm or pollution of controlled waters. Where this is the case the standard of remediation should be that which, by the use of the best practicable techniques, mitigates as far as practicable the significant harm or pollution of controlled waters which has been caused as a consequence of the existence of that linkage, or may be caused in the future as a consequence of its continued existence.

C.25   For any remediation action, package or scheme to represent the best practicable techniques, it should be implemented in accordance with best practice, including any precautions necessary to prevent damage to the environment and any other appropriate quality assurance procedures.

Multiple Pollutant Linkages

C.26   Where more than one significant pollutant linkage has been identified on the land, it may be possible to achieve the necessary overall standard of remediation for the relevant land or waters as a whole by considering what remediation actions would form part of the appropriate remediation package for each linkage (i.e., representing the best practicable techniques of remediation for that linkage) if it were the only such linkage, and then carrying out all of these remediation actions.

C.27   However, the enforcing authority should also consider whether there is an alternative remediation scheme which would, by dealing with the linkages together, be cheaper or otherwise more practicable to implement. If such a scheme can be identified which achieves an equivalent standard of remediation with respect to all of the significant pollutant linkages to which it is referable, the authority should prefer that alternative scheme.

Volunteered Remediation

C.28   In some cases, the person carrying out remediation may wish to adopt an alternative remediation scheme to that which could be required in a remediation notice. This might occur, in particular, if the person concerned wished also to prepare the land for redevelopment. The enforcing authority should consider such a remediation scheme as appropriate remediation provided the scheme would achieve at least the same standard of remediation with respect to each of the significant pollutant linkages identified on the land as would be achieved by the remediation scheme which the authority would otherwise specify in a remediation notice.

PART 5   THE REASONABLENESS OF REMEDIATION

C.29   The statutory guidance in this Part is issued under section 78E(5)(c) and provides guidance on the determination by the enforcing authority of what remediation is, or is not, to be regarded as reasonable having regard to the cost which is likely to be involved and the seriousness of the harm or of the pollution of controlled waters to which it relates.

C.30　The enforcing authority should regard a remediation action as being reasonable for the purpose of section 78E(4) if an assessment of the costs likely to be involved and of the resulting benefits shows that those benefits justify incurring those costs. Such an assessment should include the preparation of an estimate of the costs likely to be involved and of a statement of the benefits likely to result. This latter statement need not necessarily attempt to ascribe a financial value to these benefits.

C.31　For these purposes, the enforcing authority should regard the benefits resulting from a remediation action as being the contribution that the action makes, either on its own or in conjunction with other remediation actions, to:

　　(a)　reducing the seriousness of any harm or pollution of controlled waters which might otherwise be caused; or

　　(b)　mitigating the seriousness of any effects of any significant harm or pollution of controlled waters.

C.32　In assessing the reasonableness of any remediation, the enforcing authority should make due allowance for the fact that the timing of expenditure and the realisation of benefits is relevant to the balance of costs and benefits. In particular, the assessment should recognise that:

　　(a)　expenditure which is delayed to a future date will have a lesser impact on the person defraying it than would an equivalent cash sum to be spent immediately;

　　(b)　there may be a gain from achieving benefits earlier but this may also involve extra expenditure; the authority should consider whether the gain justifies the extra costs. This applies, in particular, where natural processes, managed or otherwise, would over time bring about remediation; and

　　(c)　there may be evidence that the same benefits will be achievable in the foreseeable future at a significantly lower cost, for example, through the development of new techniques or as part of a wider scheme of development or redevelopment.

C.33　The identity or financial standing of any person who may be required to pay for any remediation action are not relevant factors in the determination of whether the costs of that action are, or are not, reasonable for the purposes of section 78E(4). (These factors may however be relevant in deciding whether or not the enforcing authority can impose the cost of remediation on that person, either through the service of a remediation notice or through the recovery of costs incurred by the authority; see section 78P and the guidance in Chapter E.)

THE COST OF REMEDIATION

C.34　When considering the costs likely to be involved in carrying out any remediation action, the enforcing authority should take into account:

　　(a)　all the initial costs (including tax payable) of carrying out the remediation action, including feasibility studies, design, specification and management, as well as works and operations, and making good afterwards;

　　(b)　any on-going costs of managing and maintaining the remediation action; and

(c)   any relevant disruption costs.

C.35   For these purposes, 'relevant disruption costs' mean depreciation in the value of land or other interests, or other loss or damage, which is likely to result from the carrying out of the remediation action in question. The enforcing authority should assess these costs as their estimate of the amount of compensation which would be payable if the owner of the land or other interest had granted rights under section 78G(2) to permit the action to be carried out and had claimed compensation under section 78G(5) and regulation 6 of the Contaminated Land (England) Regulations 2000 (whether or not such a claim could actually be made).

C.36   Each of the types of cost set out in paragraph C.34 above should be included even where they would not result in payments to others by the person carrying out the remediation. For example, a company may choose to use its own staff or equipment to carry out the remediation, or the person carrying out the remediation may already own the land in question and would therefore not be entitled to receive compensation under section 78G(5). The evaluation of the cost involved in remediation should not be affected by the identity of the person carrying it out, or internal resources available to that person.

C.37   The enforcing authority should furthermore regard it as a necessary condition of an action being reasonable that:

(a)   where two or more significant pollutant linkages have been identified on the land in question, and the remediation action forms part of a wider remediation scheme which is dealing with two or more of those linkages, there is no alternative scheme which would achieve the same purposes for a lower overall cost; and

(b)   subject to subparagraph (a) above, where the remediation action forms part of a remediation package dealing with any particular significant pollutant linkage, there is no alternative package which would achieve the same standard of remediation at a lower overall cost.

C.38   In addition, for any remediation action to be reasonable there should be no alternative remediation action which would achieve the same purpose, as part of any wider remediation package or scheme, to the same standard for a lower cost (bearing in mind that the purpose of any remediation action may relate to more than one significant pollutant linkage).

THE SERIOUSNESS OF HARM OR OF POLLUTION OF CONTROLLED WATERS

C.39   When evaluating the seriousness of any significant harm, for the purposes of assessing the reasonableness of any remediation, the enforcing authority should consider:

(a)   whether the significant harm is already being caused;

(b)   the degree of the possibility of the significant harm being caused;

(c)   the nature of the significant harm with respect, in particular, to:

(i)   the nature and importance of the receptor,

(ii)   the extent and type of any effects on that receptor of the significant harm,

(iii)   the number of receptors which might be affected, and

(iv)   whether the effects would be irreversible; and

(d)   the context in which the effects might occur, in particular:

(i)   whether the receptor has already been damaged by other means and, if so, whether further effects resulting from the harm would materially affect its condition, and

(ii)   the relative risk associated with the harm in the context of wider environmental risks.

C.40   Where the significant harm is an 'ecological system effect' as defined in Chapter A, the enforcing authority should take into account any advice received from English Nature.

C.41   In evaluating for this purpose the seriousness of any pollution of controlled waters, the enforcing authority should consider:

(a)   whether the pollution of controlled waters is already being caused;

(b)   the likelihood of the pollution of controlled waters being caused;

(c)   the nature of the pollution of controlled waters involved with respect, in particular, to:

(i)   the nature and importance of the controlled waters which might be affected,

(ii)   the extent of the effects of the actual or likely pollution on those controlled waters, and

(iii)   whether such effects would be irreversible; and

(d)   the context in which the effects might occur, in particular:

(i)   whether the waters have already been polluted by other means and, if so, whether further effects resulting from the water pollution would materially affect their condition, and

(ii)   the relative risk associated with the water pollution in the context of wider environmental risks.

C.42   Where the enforcing authority is the local authority, it should take into account any advice received from the Environment Agency when it is considering the seriousness of any pollution of controlled waters.

C.43   In some instances, it may be possible to express the benefits of addressing the harm or pollution of controlled waters in direct financial terms. For example, removing a risk of explosion which renders a building unsafe for occupation could be considered to create a benefit equivalent to the cost of acquiring a replacement building. Various Government departments have produced technical advice, which the enforcing authority may find useful, on the consideration of non-market impacts of environmental matters.

PART 6   THE PRACTICABILITY, EFFECTIVENESS AND DURABILITY OF REMEDIATION

C.44   The statutory guidance in this Part is issued under section 78E(5)(b) and is relevant to the guidance given in Part 4 on the standard to which land and waters should be remediated.

GENERAL CONSIDERATIONS

C.45   In some instances, there may be little firm information on which to assess particular remediation actions, packages or schemes. For example, a particular technology or technique may not have been subject previously to field-scale pilot testing in circumstances comparable to those to be found on the contaminated land in question.

Where this is the case, the enforcing authority should consider the effectiveness and durability which it appears likely that any such action would achieve, and the practicability of its use, on the basis of information which it does have at that time (for example information derived from laboratory or other 'treatability' testing).

C.46   If the person who will be carrying out the remediation proposes the use of an innovative approach to remediation, the enforcing authority should be prepared to agree to that approach being used (subject to that person obtaining any other necessary permits or authorisations), notwithstanding the fact that there is little available information on the basis of which the authority can assess its likely effectiveness. If the approach to remediation proves to be ineffective, further remediation actions may be required, for which the person proposing the innovative approach will be liable.

C.47   However, the enforcing authority should not, under the terms of a remediation notice, require any innovative remediation action to be carried out for the purposes of establishing its effectiveness in general, unless either the person carrying out the remediation agrees or there is clear evidence that it is likely that the action would be effective on the relevant land or waters and it would meet all other requirements of the statutory guidance in this Chapter.

THE PRACTICABILITY OF REMEDIATION

C.48   The enforcing authority should consider any remediation as being practicable to the extent that it can be carried out in the circumstances of the relevant land or waters. This applies both to the remediation scheme as a whole and the individual remediation actions of which it is comprised.

C.49   In assessing the practicability of any remediation, the enforcing authority should consider, in particular, the following factors:

(a)   technical constraints, for example whether:

(i)   any technologies or other physical resources required (for example power or materials) are commercially available, or could reasonably be made available, on the necessary scale, and

(ii)   the separate remediation actions required could be carried out given the other remediation actions to be carried out, and without preventing those other actions from being carried out;

(b)   site constraints, for example whether:

(i)   the location of and access to the relevant land or waters, and the presence of buildings or other structures in, on or under the land, would permit the relevant remediation actions to be carried out in practice, and

(ii)   the remediation could be carried out, given the physical or other condition of the relevant land or waters, for example the presence of substances, whether these are part of other pollutant linkages or are not pollutants;

(c)   time constraints, for example whether it would be possible to carry out the remediation within the necessary time period given the time needed by the person carrying out the remediation to:

(i)   obtain any necessary regulatory permits and constraints, and

(ii)   design and implement the various remediation actions; and

(d)   regulatory constraints, for example whether:

(i)   the remediation can be carried out within the requirements of statutory controls relating to health and safety (including engineering safety) and pollution control,

(ii)   any necessary regulatory permits or consents would reasonably be expected to be forthcoming,

(iii)   any conditions attached to such permits or consents would affect the practicability or cost of the remediation, and

(iv)   adverse environmental impacts may arise from carrying out the remediation (see paragraphs C.51 to C.57 below).

C.50   The responsibility for obtaining any regulatory permits or consents necessary for the remediation to be carried out rests with the person who will actually be carrying out the remediation, and not with the enforcing authority. However, the authority may in some circumstances have particular duties to contribute to health and safety in the remediation work, under the Construction (Design and Management) Regulations 1994 (S.I. 1994/3140).

Adverse Environmental Impacts

C.51   Although the objective of any remediation is to improve the environment, the process of carrying out remediation may, in some circumstances, create adverse environmental impacts. The possibility of such impacts may affect the determination of what remediation package represents the best practicable techniques for remediation.

C.52   Specific pollution control permits or authorisations may be needed for some kinds of remediation processes, for example:

(a)   authorisations under Part I of the Environmental Protection Act 1990 (Integrated Pollution Control and Local Authority Air Pollution Control);

(b)   site or mobile plant licences under Part II of the Environmental Protection Act 1990 (waste management licensing); or

(c)   abstraction licences under Part II, or discharge consents under Part III, of the Water Resources Act 1991.

C.53   Permits or authorisations of these kinds may include conditions controlling the manner in which the remediation is to be carried out, intended to prevent or minimise adverse environmental impacts. Where this is the case, the enforcing authority should assume that these conditions provide a suitable level of protection for the environment.

C.54   Where this is not the case, the enforcing authority should consider whether the particular remediation package can be carried out without damaging the environment, and in particular:

(a)   without risk to water, air, soil and plants and animals;

(b)   without causing a nuisance through noise or odours;

(c)   without adversely affecting the countryside or places of special interest; and

(d)   without adversely affecting a building of special architectural or historic interest (that is, a building listed under town and country planning legislation or a building in a designated Conservation Area) or a site of archaeological interest (as defined in article 1(2) of the Town and Country Planning (General Permitted Development) Order 1995).

C.55   If the enforcing authority considers that there is some risk that the remediation might damage the environment, it should consider whether:

(a)   the risk is sufficiently great to mean that the balance of advantage, in terms of improving and protecting the environment, would lie with adopting an alternative approach to remediation, even though such an alternative may not fully achieve the objectives for remediation set out at paragraph C.18 above; or

(b)   the risk can be sufficiently reduced by including, as part of the description of what is to be done by way of remediation, particular precautions designed to prevent the occurrence of such damage to the environment (for example, precautions analogous to the conditions attached to a waste management licence).

C.56   In addition, the enforcing authority should consider whether it is likely that the process of remediation might lead to a direct or indirect discharge into groundwater of a substance in either List I or List II of the Schedule to the Groundwater Regulations 1998 (S.I. 1998/1006). (For these purposes, the terms direct discharge, indirect discharge and groundwater have the meanings given to them in the 1998 Regulations.)

C.57   If the enforcing authority considers that such a discharge is likely, it should (where that authority is not the Environment Agency) consult the Environment Agency, and have regard to its advice on whether an alternative remediation package should be adopted or precaution required as to the way that remediation is carried out.

THE EFFECTIVENESS OF REMEDIATION

C.58   The enforcing authority should consider any remediation as being effective to the extent to which the remediation scheme as a whole, and its component remediation packages, would achieve the aims set out in paragraph C.18 above in relation to each of the significant pollutant linkages identified on the relevant land or waters. The enforcing authority should consider also the extent to which each remediation action, or group of actions required for the same particular purpose, would achieve the purpose for which it was required.

C.59   Within this context, the enforcing authority should consider also the time which would pass before the remediation would become effective. In particular, the authority should establish whether the remediation would become effective sufficiently soon to match the particular degree of urgency resulting from the nature of the significant pollutant linkage in question. However, the authority may also need to balance the speed in reaching a given level of effectiveness against higher degrees of effectiveness which may be achievable, but after a longer period of time, by the use of other remediation methods.

C.60   If any remedial treatment action representing the best practicable techniques will not fully achieve the standard set out in paragraph C. 18 above, the enforcing authority should consider whether additional monitoring actions should be required.

THE DURABILITY OF REMEDIATION

C.61   The enforcing authority should consider a remediation scheme as being sufficiently durable to the extent that the scheme as a whole would continue to be effective with respect to the aims in paragraph C.18 above during the time over which the significant pollutant linkage would otherwise continue to exist or recur. Where other action (such as redevelopment) is likely to resolve or control the problem within that time, a shorter period may be appropriate. The durability of an individual remediation action is a measure of the extent to which it will continue to be effective in meeting the purpose for which it is to be required taking into account normal maintenance and repair.

C.62   Where a remediation scheme cannot reasonably and practicably continue to be effective during the whole of the expected duration of the problem, the enforcing authority should require the remediation to continue to be effective for as long as can reasonably and practicably be achieved. In these circumstances, additional monitoring actions may be required.

C.63   Where a remediation method requires on-going management and maintenance in order to continue to be effective (for example, the maintenance of gas venting or alarm systems), these on-going requirements should be specified in any remediation notice as well as any monitoring actions necessary to keep the effectiveness of the remediation under review.

PART 7   WHAT IS TO BE DONE BY WAY OF REMEDIATION

C.64   The statutory guidance in this Part is issued under section 78E(5)(a) and provides guidance on the determination by the enforcing authority of what is to be done by way of remediation — in particular, on the circumstances in which any action within the three categories of remediation action (that is, assessment, remedial treatment and monitoring actions) should be required.

ASSESSMENT ACTION

C.65   The enforcing authority should require an assessment action to be carried out where this is necessary for the purpose of obtaining information on the condition of the relevant land or waters which is needed:

(a)   to characterise in detail a significant pollutant linkage (or more than one such linkage) identified on the relevant land or waters for the purpose of enabling the authority to establish what would need to be achieved by any remedial treatment action;

(b)   to enable the establishment of the technical specifications or design of any particular remedial treatment action which the authority reasonably considers it might subsequently require to be carried out; or

(c)   where, after remedial treatment actions have been carried out, the land will still be in such a condition that it would still fall to be identified as contaminated land, to evaluate the condition of the relevant land or waters, or the incidence of any significant harm or pollution of controlled waters, for the purpose of supporting future decisions on whether further remediation might then be required (this applies where the remediation action concerned would not otherwise constitute a monitoring action).

C.66   The enforcing authority should not require any assessment action to be carried out unless that action is needed to achieve one or more of the purposes set out in paragraph C.65 above, and it represents a reasonable means of doing so. In particular, no assessment action should be required for the purposes of determining whether or not the land in question is contaminated land. For the purposes of this guidance, assessment actions relate solely to land which has already been formally identified as contaminated land, or to other land or waters which might be affected by it. The statutory guidance in Chapters A and B sets out the requirements for the inspection of land and the manner in which a local authority should determine that land appears to it to be contaminated land.

REMEDIAL TREATMENT ACTION

C.67   The enforcing authority should require a remedial treatment action to be carried out where it is necessary to achieve the standard of remediation described in Part 4, but for no other purpose. Any such remedial treatment action should include appropriate verification measures. When considering what remedial treatment action may be necessary, the enforcing authority should consider also what complementary assessment or monitoring actions might be needed to evaluate the manner in which the remedial treatment action is implemented or its effectiveness or durability once implemented.

MONITORING ACTION

C.68   The enforcing authority should require a monitoring action to be carried out where it is for the purpose of providing information on any changes which might occur in the condition of a pollutant, pathway or receptor, where:

(a)   the pollutant, pathway or receptor in question was identified previously as part of a significant pollutant linkage; and

(b)   the authority will need to consider whether any further remedial treatment action will be required as a consequence of any change that may occur.

C.69   Monitoring action should not be required to achieve any other purpose, such as general monitoring to enable the enforcing authority to identify any new significant pollutant linkages which might become present in the future. This latter activity forms part of the local authority's duty, under section 78B(1), to cause its area to be inspected from time to time for the purpose of identifying any contaminated land.

WHAT REMEDIATION SHOULD NOT BE REQUIRED

C.70   The enforcing authority should not require any remediation to be carried out for the purpose of achieving any aims other than those set out in paragraphs C.18 to C.24 above, or purposes other than those identified in this Part of this Chapter. In particular, it should not require any remediation to be carried out for the purposes of:

(a)   dealing with matters which do not in themselves form part of a significant pollutant linkage, such as substances present in quantities or concentrations at which there is neither a significant possibility of significant harm being caused nor a likelihood of any pollution of controlled waters being caused; or

(b)   making the land suitable for any uses other than its current use, as defined in paragraphs A.25 and A.26 in Chapter A.

C.71 It is, however, always open to the owner of the land, or any other person who might be liable for remediation, to carry out on a voluntary basis remediation to meet these wider objectives.

CHAPTER D   STATUTORY GUIDANCE ON EXCLUSION FROM, AND APPORTIONMENT OF, LIABILITY FOR REMEDIATION

PART 1   SCOPE OF THE CHAPTER

D.1   The statutory guidance in this Chapter is issued under sections 78F(6) and 78F(7) of the Environmental Protection Act 1990. It provides guidance on circumstances where two or more persons are liable to bear the responsibility for any particular thing by way of remediation. It deals with the questions of who should be excluded from liability, and how the cost of each remediation action should be apportioned between those who remain liable after any such exclusion.

D.2   Section 78F provides that:

'(6)   Where two or more persons would, apart from this subsection, be appropriate persons in relation to any particular thing which is to be done by way of remediation, the enforcing authority shall determine in accordance with guidance issued for the purpose by the Secretary of State whether any, and if so which, of them is to be treated as not being an appropriate person in relation to that thing.

(7)   Where two or more persons are appropriate persons in relation to any particular thing which is to be done by way of remediation, they shall be liable to bear the cost of doing that thing in proportions determined by the enforcing authority in accordance with guidance issued for the purpose by the Secretary of State'.

D.3   The enforcing authority is therefore required to act in accordance with the guidance in this Chapter. Introductory summaries are included to various parts and sections of the guidance: these do not necessarily give the full detail of the guidance; the section concerned should be consulted.

PART 2   DEFINITIONS OF TERMS

D.4   Unless otherwise stated, any word, term or phrase given a specific meaning in Part IIA of the Environmental Protection Act 1990, or in the statutory guidance in Chapters A or B, has the same meaning for the purpose of the guidance in this Chapter.

D.5   In addition, for the purposes of this Chapter, the following definitions apply:

(a)   a person who is an appropriate person by virtue of section 78F(2) (that is, because he has caused or knowingly permitted a pollutant to be in, on or under the land) is described as a 'Class A person';

(b)   a person who is an appropriate person by virtue of section 78F(4) or (5) (that is, because he is the owner or occupier of the land in circumstances where no Class A person can be found with respect to a particular remediation action) is described as a 'Class B person';

(c)   collectively, the persons who are appropriate persons with respect to any particular significant pollutant linkage are described as the 'liability group' for that linkage; a liability group consisting of one or more Class A persons is described as a 'Class A liability group', and a liability group consisting of one or more Class B persons is described as a 'Class B liability group';

(d)   any determination by the enforcing authority under section 78F(6) (that is, a person is to be treated as not being an appropriate person) is described as an 'exclusion';

(e)   any determination by the enforcing authority under section 78F(7) (dividing the costs of carrying out any remediation action between two or more appropriate persons) is described as an 'apportionment'; the process of apportionment between liability groups is described as 'attribution';

(f)   a 'remediation action' is any individual thing which is being, or is to be, done by way of remediation;

(g)   a 'remediation package' is all the remediation actions, within a remediation scheme, which are referable to a particular significant pollutant linkage; and

(h)   a 'remediation scheme' is the complete set or sequence of remediation actions (referable to one or more significant pollutant linkages) to be carried out with respect to the relevant land or waters.

D.6   Any reference to 'Part IIA' means 'Part IIA of the Environmental Protection Act 1990'. Any reference to a 'section' in primary legislation means a section of the Environmental Protection Act 1990, unless it is specifically stated otherwise.

PART 3   THE PROCEDURE FOR DETERMINING LIABILITIES

D.7   For most sites, the process of determining liabilities will consist simply of identifying either a single person (either an individual or a corporation such as a limited company) who has caused or knowingly permitted the presence of a single significant pollutant, or the owner of the site. The history of other sites may be more complex. A succession of different occupiers or of different industries, or a variety of substances may all have contributed to the problems which have made the land 'contaminated land' as defined for the purposes of Part IIA. Numerous separate remediation actions may be required, which may not correlate neatly with those who are to bear responsibility for the costs. The degree of responsibility for the state of the land may vary widely. Determining liability for the costs of each remediation action can be correspondingly complex.

D.8   The statutory guidance in this Part sets out the procedure which the enforcing authority should follow for determining which appropriate persons should bear what responsibility for each remediation action. It refers forward to the other Parts of this Chapter, and describes how they should be applied. Not all stages will be relevant to all cases, particularly where there is only a single significant pollutant linkage, or where a liability group has only one member.

FIRST STAGE — IDENTIFYING POTENTIAL APPROPRIATE PERSONS AND LIABILITY GROUPS

D.9   As part of the process of determining that the land is 'contaminated land' (see Chapters A and B), the enforcing authority will have identified at least one significant pollutant linkage (pollutant, pathway and receptor), resulting from the presence of at least one significant pollutant.

Where there is a Single Significant Pollutant Linkage

D.10   The enforcing authority should identify all of the persons who would be appropriate persons to pay for any remediation action which is referable to the pollutant which forms part of the significant pollutant linkage. These persons constitute the 'liability group' for that significant pollutant linkage. (In this guidance the term 'liability group' is used even where there is only a single appropriate person who is a 'member' of the liability group.)

D.11   To achieve this, the enforcing authority should make reasonable enquiries to find all those who have caused or knowingly permitted the pollutant in question to be in, on or under the land. Any such persons constitute a 'Class A liability group' for the significant pollutant linkage.

D.12   If no such Class A persons can be found for any significant pollutant, the enforcing authority should consider whether the significant pollutant linkage of which it forms part relates solely to the pollution of controlled waters, rather than to any significant harm. If this is the case, there will be no liability group for that significant pollutant linkage, and it should be treated as an 'orphan linkage' (see paragraphs D.103 to D.109 below).

D.13   In any other case where no Class A persons can be found for a significant pollutant, the enforcing authority should identify all of the current owners or occupiers of the contaminated land in question. These persons then constitute a 'Class B liability group' for the significant pollutant linkage.

D.14   If the enforcing authority cannot find any Class A persons or any Class B persons in respect of a significant pollutant linkage, there will be no liability group for that linkage and it should be treated as an orphan linkage (see paragraphs D.103 to D.109 below).

Where there are Two or More Significant Pollutant Linkages

D.15   The enforcing authority should consider each significant pollutant linkage in turn, carrying out the steps set out in paragraphs D.10 to D.14 above, in order to identify the liability group (if one exists) for each of the linkages.

In All Cases

D.16   Having identified one or more liability groups, the enforcing authority should consider whether any of the members of those groups are exempted from liability under the provisions in Part IIA. This could apply where:

(a)   a person who would otherwise be a Class A person is exempted from liability arising with respect to water pollution from an abandoned mine (see section 78J(3));

(b)   a Class B person is exempted from liability arising from the escape of a pollutant from one piece of land to other land (see section 78K); or

(c)   a person is exempted from liability by virtue of his being a person 'acting in a relevant capacity' (such as acting as an insolvency practitioner), as defined in section 78X(4).

D.17   If all of the members of any liability group benefit from one or more of these exemptions, the enforcing authority should treat the significant pollutant linkage in question as an orphan linkage (see paragraphs D.103 to D.109 below).

D.18   Persons may be members of more than one liability group. This might apply, for example, if they caused or knowingly permitted the presence of more than one significant pollutant.

D.19   Where the membership of all of the liability groups is the same, there may be opportunities for the enforcing authority to abbreviate the remaining stages of this procedure. However, the tests for exclusion and apportionment may produce different results for different significant pollutant linkages, and so the enforcing authority should exercise caution before trying to simplify the procedure in any case.

SECOND STAGE — CHARACTERISING REMEDIATION ACTIONS

D.20   Each remediation action will be carried out to achieve a particular purpose with respect to one or more defined significant pollutant linkages. Where there is a single significant pollutant linkage on the land in question, all the remediation actions will be referable to that linkage, and there is no need to consider how the different actions relate to different linkages. This stage and the third stage of the procedure therefore do not need to be carried out in where there is only a single significant pollutant linkage.

D.21   However, where there are two or more significant pollutant linkages on the land in question, the enforcing authority should establish whether each remediation action is:

(a)   referable solely to the significant pollutant in a single significant pollutant linkage (a 'single-linkage action'); or

(b)   referable to the significant pollutant in more than one significant pollutant linkage (a 'shared action').

D.22   Where a remediation action is a shared action, there are two possible relationships between it and the significant pollutant linkages to which it is referable. The enforcing authority should establish whether the shared action is:

(a)   a 'common action' — that is, an action which addresses together all of the significant pollutant linkages to which it is referable, and which would have been part of the remediation package for each of those linkages if each of them had been addressed separately; or

(b)   a 'collective action' — that is, an action which addresses together all of the significant pollutant linkages to which it is referable, but which would not have been part of the remediation package for every one of those linkages if each of them had been addressed separately, because:

(i)   the action would not have been appropriate in that form for one or more of the linkages (since some different solution would have been more appropriate),

(ii)   the action would not have been needed to the same extent for one or more of the linkages (since a less far-reaching version of that type of action would have sufficed), or

(iii)   the action represents a more economic way of addressing the linkages together which would not be possible if they were addressed separately.

D.23   A collective action replaces actions that would have been appropriate for the individual significant pollutant linkages if they had been addressed separately, as it achieves the purposes which those other actions would have achieved.

THIRD STAGE — ATTRIBUTING RESPONSIBILITY BETWEEN LIABILITY GROUPS

D.24   This stage of the procedure does not apply in the simpler cases. Where there is only a single significant pollutant linkage, the liability group for that linkage bears the full cost of carrying out any remediation action. (Where the linkage is an orphan linkage, the enforcing authority has the power to carry out the remediation action itself, at its own cost.)

D.25   Similarly, for any single-linkage action, the liability group for the significant pollutant linkage in question bears the full cost of carrying out that action.

D.26   However, the enforcing authority should apply the guidance in Part 9 with respect to each shared action, in order to attribute to each of the different liability groups their share of responsibility for that action.

D.27   After the guidance in Part 9 has been applied to all shared actions, it may be the case that a Class B liability group which has been identified does not have to bear the costs for any remediation actions. Where this is the case, the enforcing authority does not need to apply any of the rest of the guidance in this Chapter to that liability group.

FOURTH STAGE — EXCLUDING MEMBERS OF A LIABILITY GROUP

D.28   The enforcing authority should now consider, for each liability group which has two or more members, whether any of those members should be excluded from liability:

(a)   for each Class A liability group with two or more members, the enforcing authority should apply the guidance on exclusion in Part 5; and

(b)   for each Class B liability group with two or more members, the enforcing authority should apply the guidance on exclusion in Part 7.

FIFTH STAGE — APPORTIONING LIABILITY BETWEEN MEMBERS OF A LIABILITY GROUP

D.29   The enforcing authority should now determine how any costs attributed to each liability group should be apportioned between the members of that group who remain after any exclusions have been made.

D.30   For any liability group which has only a single remaining member, that person bears all of the costs falling to that liability group, that is both the cost of any single-linkage action referable to the significant pollutant linkage in question, and the share of the cost of any shared action attributed to the group as a result of the attribution process set out in Part 9.

D.31   For any liability group which has two or more remaining members, the enforcing authority should apply the relevant guidance on apportionment between those members. Each of the remaining members of the group will then bear the proportion determined under that guidance of the total costs falling to the group, that is both the cost of any single-linkage action referable to the significant pollutant linkage in question, and the share of the cost of any shared action attributed to the group as a result of the attribution process set out in Part 9. The relevant apportionment guidance is:

(a)   for any Class A liability group, the guidance set out in Part 6; and

(b)   for any Class B liability group, the guidance set out in Part 8.

PART 4   GENERAL CONSIDERATIONS RELATING TO THE EXCLUSION, APPORTIONMENT AND ATTRIBUTION PROCEDURES

D.32   This Part sets out general guidance about the application of the exclusion, apportionment and attribution procedures set out in the rest of this Chapter. It is accordingly issued under both section 78F(6) and section 78F(7).

D.33   The enforcing authority should ensure that any person who might benefit from an exclusion, apportionment or attribution is aware of the guidance in this Chapter, so that they may make appropriate representations to the enforcing authority.

D.34　The enforcing authority should apply the tests for exclusion (in Parts 5 and 7) with respect to the members of each liability group. If a person, who would otherwise be an appropriate person to bear responsibility for a particular remediation action, has been excluded from the liability groups for all of the significant pollutant linkages to which that action is referable, he should be treated as not being an appropriate person in relation to that remediation action.

FINANCIAL CIRCUMSTANCES

D.35　The financial circumstances of those concerned should have no bearing on the application of the procedures for exclusion, apportionment and attribution in this Chapter, except where the circumstances in paragraph D.85 below apply (the financial circumstances of those concerned are taken into account in the separate consideration under section 78P(2) on hardship and cost recovery). In particular, it should be irrelevant in the context of decisions on exclusion and apportionment:

(a)　whether those concerned would benefit from any limitation on the recovery of costs under the provisions on hardship and cost recovery in section 78P(2); or

(b)　whether those concerned would benefit from any insurance or other means of transferring their responsibilities to another person.

INFORMATION AND DECISIONS

D.36　The enforcing authority should make reasonable endeavours to consult those who may be affected by any exclusion, apportionment or attribution. In all cases, however, it should seek to obtain only such information as it is reasonable to seek, having regard to:

(a)　how the information might be obtained;

(b)　the cost of obtaining the information for all parties involved; and

(c)　the potential significance of the information for any decision.

D.37 The statutory guidance in this Chapter should be applied in the light of the circumstances as they appear to the enforcing authority on the basis of the evidence available to it at that time. The enforcing authority's judgements should be made on the basis of the balance of probabilities. The enforcing authority should take into account the information that it has acquired in the light of the guidance in the previous paragraph, but the burden of providing the authority with any further information needed to establish an exclusion or to influence an apportionment or attribution should rest on any person seeking such a benefit. The enforcing authority should consider any relevant information which has been provided by those potentially liable under these provisions. Where any such person provides such information, any other person who may be affected by an exclusion, apportionment or attribution based on that information should be given a reasonable opportunity to comment on that information before the determination is made.

AGREEMENTS ON LIABILITIES

D.38   In any case where:

(a)   two or more persons are appropriate persons and thus responsible for all or part of the costs of a remediation action;

(b)   they agree, or have agreed, the basis on which they wish to divide that responsibility; and

(c)   a copy of the agreement is provided to the enforcing authority and none of the parties to the agreement informs the authority that it challenges the application of the agreement;

the enforcing authority should generally make such determinations on exclusion, apportionment and attribution as are needed to give effect to this agreement, and should not apply the remainder of this guidance for exclusion, apportionment or attribution between the parties to the agreement. However, the enforcing authority should apply the guidance to determine any exclusions, apportionments or attributions between any or all of those parties and any other appropriate persons who are not parties to the agreement.

D.39   However, where giving effect to such an agreement would increase the share of the costs theoretically to be borne by a person who would benefit from a limitation on recovery of remediation costs under the provision on hardship in section 78P(2) (a) or under the guidance on cost recovery issued under section 78P(2)(b), the enforcing authority should disregard the agreement.

PART 5   EXCLUSION OF MEMBERS OF A CLASS A LIABILITY GROUP

D.40   The guidance in this Part is issued under section 78F(6) and, with respect to effects of the exclusion tests on apportionment (see paragraph D.43 below in particular), under section 78F(7). It sets out the tests for determining whether to exclude from liability a person who would otherwise be a Class A person (that is, a person who has been identified as responsible for remediation costs by reason of his having 'caused or knowingly permitted' the presence of a significant pollutant). The tests are intended to establish whether, in relation to other members of the liability group, it is fair that he should bear any part of that responsibility.

D.41   The exclusion tests in this Part are subject to the following overriding guidance:

(a)   the exclusions that the enforcing authority should make are solely in respect of the significant pollutant linkage giving rise to the liability of the liability group in question., an exclusion in respect of one significant pollutant linkage has no necessary implication in respect to any other such linkage, and a person who has been excluded with respect to one linkage may still be liable to meet all or part of the cost of carrying out a remediation action by reason of his membership of another liability group;

(b)   the tests should be applied in the sequence in which they are set out; and

(c)   if the result of applying a test would be to exclude all of the members of the liability group who remain after any exclusions resulting from previous tests, that further test should not be applied, and consequently the related exclusions should not be made.

D.42   The effect of any exclusion made under Test 1, or Tests 4 to 6 below should be to remove completely any liability that would otherwise have fallen on the person benefiting from the exclusion. Where the enforcing authority makes any exclusion under one of these tests, it should therefore apply any subsequent exclusion tests, and make any apportionment within the liability group, in the same way as it would have done if the excluded person had never been a member of the liability group.

D.43   The effect of any exclusion made under Test 2 ('Payments Made for Remediation') or Test 3 ('Sold with Information'), on the other hand, is intended to be that the person who received the payment or bought the land, as the case may be, (the 'payee or buyer') should bear the liability of the person excluded (the 'payer or seller') in addition to any liability which he is to bear in respect of his own actions or omissions. To achieve this, the enforcing authority should:

(a)   complete the application of the other exclusion tests and then apportion liability between the members of the liability group, as if the payer or seller were not excluded as a result of Test 2 or Test 3; and

(b)   then apportion any liability of the payer or seller, calculated on this hypothetical basis, to the payee or buyer, in addition to the liability (if any) that the payee or buyer has in respect of his own actions or omissions; this should be done even if the payee or buyer would otherwise have been excluded from the liability group by one of the other exclusion tests.

RELATED COMPANIES

D.44   Before applying any of the exclusion tests, the enforcing authority should establish whether two or more of the members of the liability group are 'related companies'.

D.45   Where the question to be considered in any exclusion test concerns the relationship between, or the relative positions of, two or more related companies, the enforcing authority should not apply the test so as to exclude any of the related companies. For example, in Test 3 ('Sold with Information'), if the 'seller' and the 'buyer' are related companies, the 'seller' would not be excluded by virtue of that Test.

D.46   For these purposes, 'related companies' are those which are, or were at the 'relevant date', members of a group of companies consisting of a 'holding company' and its 'subsidiaries'. The 'relevant date' is that on which the enforcing authority first served on anyone a notice under section 78B(3) identifying the land as contaminated land, and the terms 'holding company' and 'subsidiaries' have the same meaning as in section 736 of the Companies Act 1985.

THE EXCLUSION TESTS FOR CLASS A PERSONS

Test 1 — 'Excluded Activities'

D.47   The purpose of this test is to exclude those who have been identified as having caused or knowingly permitted the land to be contaminated land solely by reason of having carried out certain activities. The activities are ones which, in the Government's view, carry such limited responsibility, if any, that exclusion would be justified even where the activity is held to amount to 'causing or knowingly permitting' under Part IIA. It does not imply that the carrying out of such activities necessarily amounts to 'causing or knowingly permitting'.

D.48 In applying this test with respect to any appropriate person, the enforcing authority should consider whether the person in question is a member of a liability group solely by reason of one or more of the following activities (not including any associated activity outside these descriptions):

(a)   providing (or withholding) financial assistance to another person (whether or not that other person is a member of the liability group), in the form of any one or more of the following:

(i)   making a grant,

(ii)   making a loan or providing any other form of credit, including instalment credit, leasing arrangements and mortgages,

(iii)   guaranteeing the performance of a person's obligations,

(iv)   indemnifying a person in respect of any loss, liability or damage,

(v)   investing in the undertaking of a body corporate by acquiring share capital or loan capital of that body without thereby acquiring such control as a 'holding company' has over a 'subsidiary' as defined in section 736 of the Companies Act 1985, or

(vi)   providing a person with any other financial benefit (including the remission in whole or in part of any financial liability or obligation);

(b)   underwriting an insurance policy under which another person was insured in respect of any occurrence, condition or omission by reason of which that other person has been held to have caused or knowingly permitted the significant pollutant to be in, on or under the land in question; for the purposes of this sub-paragraph:

(i)   under-writing an insurance policy is to be taken to include imposing any conditions on the person insured, for example relating to the manner in which he carries out the insured activity, and

(ii)   it is irrelevant whether or not the insured person can now be found;

(c)   as a provider of financial assistance or as an underwriter, carrying out any action for the purpose of deciding whether or not to provide such financial assistance or underwrite such an insurance policy as is mentioned above; this subparagraph does not apply to the carrying out of any intrusive investigation in respect of the land in question for the purpose of making that decision where:

(i)   the carrying out of that investigation is itself a cause of the existence, nature or continuance of the significant pollutant linkage in question, and

(ii)   the person who applied for the financial assistance or insurance is not a member of the liability group;

(d)   consigning, as waste, to another person the substance which is now a significant pollutant, under a contract under which that other person knowingly took over responsibility for its proper disposal or other management on a site not under the control of the person seeking to be excluded from liability; (for the purpose of this sub-paragraph, it is irrelevant whether or not the person to whom the waste was consigned can now be found);

(e)   creating at any time a tenancy over the land in question in favour of another person who has subsequently caused or knowingly permitted the presence of the significant pollutant linkage in question (whether or not the tenant can now be found);

(f)   as owner of the land in question, licensing at any time its occupation by another person who has subsequently caused or knowingly permitted the presence of the significant pollutant in question (whether or not the licensee can now be found); this test does not apply in a case where the person granting the licence operated the land as a site for the disposal or storage of waste at the time of the grant of the licence;

(g)   issuing any statutory permission, licence or consent required for any action or omission by reason of which some other person appears to the enforcing authority to have caused or knowingly permitted the presence of the significant pollutant in question (whether or not that other person can now be found); this test does not apply in the case of statutory undertakers granting permission for their contractors to carry out works;

(h)   taking, or not taking, any statutory enforcement action:

(i)   with respect to the land, or

(ii)   against some other person who appears to the enforcing authority to have caused or knowingly permitted the presence of the significant pollutant in question, whether or not that other person can now be found;

(i)   providing legal, financial, engineering, scientific or technical advice to (or design, contract management or works management services for) another person (the 'client'), whether or not that other person can now be found:

(i)   in relation to an action or omission (or a series of actions and/or omissions) by reason of which the client has been held to have caused or knowingly permitted the presence of the significant pollutant,

(ii)   for the purpose of assessing the condition of the land, for example whether it might be contaminated, or

(iii)   for the purpose of establishing what might be done to the land by way of remediation;

(j)   as a person providing advice or services as described in sub-paragraph (i) above carrying out any intrusive investigation in respect of the land in question, except where:

(i)   the investigation is itself a cause of the existence, nature or continuance of the significant pollutant linkage in question, and

(ii)   the client is not a member of the liability group; or

(k)   performing any contract by providing a service (whether the contract is a contract of service (employment), or a contract for services) or by supplying goods, where the contract is made with another person who is also a member of the liability group in question; for the purposes of this sub-paragraph and paragraph D.49 below, the person providing the service or supplying the goods is referred to as the 'contractor' and the other party as the 'employer'; this subparagraph applies to subcontracts where either the ultimate employer or an intermediate contractor is a member of the liability group; this sub-paragraph does not apply where:

(i)   the activity under the contract is of a kind referred to in a previous sub-paragraph of this paragraph,

(ii)   the action or omission by the contractor by virtue of which he has been identified as an appropriate person was not in accordance with the terms of the contract, or

(iii)   the circumstances in paragraph D.49 below apply.

D.49   The circumstances referred to in paragraph D.48(k)(iii) are:

(a)   the employer is a body corporate;

(b)   the contractor was a director, manager, secretary or other similar officer of the body corporate, or a person purporting to act in any such capacity, at the time when the contract was performed; and

(c)   the action or omissions by virtue of which the employer has been identified as an appropriate person were carried out or made with the consent or connivance of the contractor, or were attributable to any neglect on his part.

D.50   If any of the circumstances in paragraph D.48 above apply, the enforcing authority should exclude the person in question.

Test 2 — 'Payments made for Remediation'

D.51   The purpose of this test is to exclude from liability those who have already, in effect, met their responsibilities by making certain kinds of payment to some other member of the liability group, which would have been sufficient to pay for adequate remediation.

D.52   In applying this test, the enforcing authority should consider whether all the following circumstances exist:

(a)   one of the members of the liability group has made a payment to another member of that liability group for the purpose of carrying out particular remediation on the land in question; only payments of the kinds set out in paragraph D.53 below are to be taken into account;

(b)   that payment would have been sufficient at the date when it was made to pay for the remediation in question;

(c)   if the remediation for which the payment was intended had been carried out effectively, the land in question would not now be in such a condition that it has been identified as contaminated land by reason of the significant pollutant linkage in question; and

(d)   the remediation in question was not carried out or was not carried out effectively.

D.53   Payments of the following kinds alone should be taken into account:

(a)   a payment made voluntarily, or to meet a contractual obligation, in response to a claim for the cost of the particular remediation;

(b)   · a payment made in the course of a civil legal action, or arbitration, mediation or dispute resolution procedure, covering the cost of the particular remediation, whether paid as part of an out-of-court settlement, or paid under the terms of a court order; or

(c)   a payment as part of a contract (including a group of interlinked contracts) for the transfer of ownership of the land in question which is either specifically provided for in the contract to meet the cost of carrying out the particular remediation or which consists of a reduction in the contract price explicitly stated in the contract to be for that purpose.

D.54   For the purposes of this test, payments include consideration of any form.

D.55   However, no payment should be taken into account where the person making the payment retained any control after the date of the payment over the condition of the land in question (that is, over whether or not the substances by reason of which the land is regarded as contaminated land were permitted to be in, on or under the land). For this purpose, neither of the following should be regarded as retaining control over the condition of the land:

(a)   holding contractual rights to ensure the proper carrying out of the remediation for which the payment was made; nor

(b)   holding an interest or right of any of the following kinds:

(i)   easements for the benefit of other land, where the contaminated land in question is the servient tenement, and statutory rights of an equivalent nature, rights of statutory undertakers to carry out works or install equipment,

(iii)   reversions upon expiry or termination of a long lease, or

(iv)   the benefit of restrictive covenants or equivalent statutory agreements.

D.56   If all of the circumstances set out in paragraph D.52 above apply, the enforcing authority should exclude the person who made the payment in respect of the remediation action in question. (See paragraph D.43 above for guidance on how this exclusion should be made.)

Test 3 — 'Sold with Information'

D.57   The purpose of this test is to exclude from liability those who, although they have caused or knowingly permitted the presence of a significant pollutant in, on or under some land, have disposed of that land in circumstances where it is reasonable that another member of the liability group, who has acquired the land from them, should bear the liability for remediation of the land.

D.58   In applying this test, the enforcing authority should consider whether all the following circumstances exist:

(a)   one of the members of the liability group (the 'seller') has sold the land in question to a person who is also a member of the liability group (the 'buyer');

(b)   the sale took place at arms' length (that is, on terms which could be expected in a sale on the open market between a willing seller and a willing buyer);

(c)   before the sale became binding, the buyer had information that would reasonably allow that particular person to be aware of the presence on the land of the pollutant identified in the significant pollutant linkage in question, and the broad measure of that presence; and the seller did nothing material to misrepresent the implications of that presence; and

(d)   after the date of the sale, the seller did not retain any interest in the land in question or any rights to occupy or use that land.

D.59 In determining whether these circumstances exist:

(a)   a sale of land should be regarded as being either the transfer of the freehold or the grant or assignment of a long lease; for this purpose, a 'long lease' means a lease (or sub-lease) granted for a period of more than 21 years under which the lessee satisfies the definition of 'owner' set out in section 78A(9);

(b)   the question of whether persons are members of a liability group should be decided on the circumstances as they exist at the time of the determination (and not as they might have been at the time of the sale of the land);

(c)   where there is a group of transactions or a wider agreement (such as the sale of a company or business) including a sale of land, that sale of land should be taken to have been at arms' length where the person seeking to be excluded can show that the net effect of the group of transactions or the agreement as a whole was a sale at arms' length;

(d)   in transactions since the beginning of 1990 where the buyer is a large commercial organisation or public body, permission from the seller for the buyer to carry out his own investigations of the condition of the land should normally be taken as sufficient indication that the buyer had the information referred to in paragraph D.58(c) above; and

(c)   for the purposes of paragraph D.58(d) above, the following rights should be disregarded in deciding whether the seller has retained an interest in the contaminated land in question or rights to occupy or use it:

(i)   easements for the benefit of other land, where the contaminated land in question is the servient tenement, and statutory rights of an equivalent nature,

(ii)   rights of statutory undertakers to carry out works or install equipment,

(iii)   reversions upon expiry or termination of a long lease, and

(iv)   the benefit of restrictive covenants or equivalent statutory agreements.

D.60   If all of the circumstances in paragraph D.58 above apply, the enforcing authority should exclude the seller. (See paragraph D.43 above for guidance on how this exclusion should be made.)

D.61   This test does not imply that the receipt by the buyer of the information referred to in paragraph D.58(c) above necessarily means that the buyer has 'caused or knowingly permitted' the presence of the significant pollutant in, on or under the land.

Test 4 — 'Changes to Substances'

D.62   The purpose of this test is to exclude from liability those who are members of a liability group solely because they caused or knowingly permitted the presence in, on or under the land of a substance which has only led to the creation of a significant pollutant linkage because of its interaction with another substance which was later introduced to the land by another person.

D.63   In applying this test, the enforcing authority should consider whether all the following circumstances exist:

(a)   the substance forming part of the significant pollutant linkage in question is present, or has become a significant pollutant, only as the result of a chemical reaction, biological process or other change (the 'intervening change') involving:

(i)   both a substance (the 'earlier substance') which would not have formed part of the significant pollutant linkage if the intervening change had not occurred, and

(ii)   one or more other substances (the 'later substances');

(b)   the intervening change would not have occurred in the absence of the later substances;

(c)   a person (the 'first person') is a member of the liability group because he caused or knowingly permitted the presence in, on or under the land of the earlier substance, but he did not cause or knowingly permit the presence of any of the later substances;

(d)   one or more other persons are members of the liability group because they caused or knowingly permitted the later substances to be in, on or under the land;

(e)   before the date when the later substances started to be introduced in, on or under the land, the first person:

(i)   could not reasonably have foreseen that the later substances would be introduced onto the land,

(ii)   could not reasonably have foreseen that, if they were, the intervening change would be likely to happen, or

(iii)   took what, at that date, were reasonable precautions to prevent the introduction of the later substances or the occurrence of the intervening change, even though those precautions have, in the event, proved to be inadequate; and

(f)   after that date, the first person did not:

(i)   cause or knowingly permit any more of the earlier substance to be in, on or under the land in question,

(ii)   do anything which has contributed to the conditions that brought about the intervening change, or

(iii)   fall to do something which he could reasonably have been expected to do to prevent the intervening change happening.

D.64   If all of the circumstances in paragraph D.63 above apply, the enforcing authority should exclude the first person (or persons, if more than one member of the liability group meets this description).

Test 5 — 'Escaped Substances'

D.65   The purpose of this test is to exclude from liability those who would otherwise be liable for the remediation of contaminated land which has become contaminated as a result of the escape of substances from other land, where it can be shown that another member of the liability group was actually responsible for that escape.

D.66   In applying this test, the enforcing authority should consider whether all the following circumstances exist:

(a)   a significant pollutant is present in, on or under the contaminated land in question wholly or partly as a result of its escape from other land;

(b)   a member of the liability group for the significant pollutant linkage of which that pollutant forms part:

(i)   caused or knowingly permitted the pollutant to be present in, on or under that other land (that is, he is a member, of that liability group by reason of section 78K(1)), and

(ii)   is a member of that liability group solely for that reason; and

(c)   one or more other members of that liability group caused or knowingly permitted the significant pollutant to escape from that other land and its escape would not have happened but for their actions or omissions.

D.67   If all of the circumstances in paragraph D.66 above apply, the enforcing authority should exclude any person meeting the description in paragraph D.66(b) above.

Test 6 — 'Introduction of Pathways or Receptors'

D.68   The purpose of this test is to exclude from liability those who would otherwise be liable solely because of the subsequent introduction by others of the relevant pathways or receptors (as defined in Chapter A) in the significant pollutant linkage.

D.69   In applying this test, the enforcing authority should consider whether all the following circumstances exist:

(a)   one or more members of the liability group have carried out a relevant action, and/or made a relevant omission ('the later actions'), either

(i)   as part of the series of actions and/or omissions which amount to their having caused or knowingly permitted the presence of the pollutant in a significant pollutant linkage, or

(ii)   in addition to that series of actions and/or omissions;

(b)   the effect of the later actions has been to introduce the pathway or the receptor which form part of the significant pollutant linkage in question;

(c)   if those later actions had not been carried out or made, the significant pollutant linkage would either not have existed, or would not have been a significant pollutant linkage, because of the absence of a pathway or of a receptor; and

(d)   a person is a member of the liability group in question solely by reason of his carrying out other actions or making other omissions ('the earlier actions') which were completed before any of the later actions were carried out or made.

D.70   For the purpose of this test:

(a)   a 'relevant action' means:

(i)   the carrying out at any time of building, engineering, mining or other operations in, on, over or under the land in question, and/or

(ii)   the making of any material change in the use of the land in question for which a specific application for planning permission was required to be made (as opposed to permission being granted, or deemed to be granted, by general legislation or by virtue of a development order, the adoption of a simplified planning zone or the designation of an enterprise zone) at the time when the change in use was made; and

(b)   a 'relevant omission' means:

(i)   in the course of a relevant action, failing to take a step which would have ensured that a significant pollutant linkage was not brought into existence as a result of that action, and/or (ii)　　unreasonably failing to maintain or operate a system installed for the purpose of reducing or managing the risk associated with the presence on the land in question of the significant pollutant in the significant pollutant linkage in question.

D.71　This test applies only with respect to developments on, or changes in the use of, the contaminated land itself; it does not apply where the relevant acts or omissions take place on other land, even if they have the effect of introducing pathways or receptors.

D.72　If all of the circumstances in paragraph D.69 above apply, the enforcing authority should exclude any person meeting the description at paragraph D.69(d) above.

PART 6　APPORTIONMENT BETWEEN MEMBERS OF ANY SINGLE CLASS A LIABILITY GROUP

D.73　The statutory guidance in this Part is issued under section 78F(7) and sets out the principles on which liability should be apportioned within each Class A liability group as it stands after any members have been excluded from liability with respect to the relevant significant pollutant linkage as a result of the application of the exclusion tests in Part 5.

D.74　The history and circumstances of different areas of contaminated land, and the nature of the responsibility of each of the members of any Class A liability group for a significant pollutant linkage, are likely to vary greatly. It is therefore not possible to prescribe detailed rules for the apportionment of liability between those members which would be fair and appropriate in all cases.

GENERAL PRINCIPLES

D.75　In apportioning costs between the members of a Class A liability group who remain after any exclusions have been made, the enforcing authority should follow the general principle that liability should be apportioned to reflect the relative responsibility of each of those members for creating or continuing the risk now being caused by the significant pollutant linkage in question. (For these purposes, 'risk' has the same meaning as that given in Chapter A.) In applying this principle, the enforcing authority should follow, where appropriate, the specific approaches set out in paragraphs D.77 to D.86 below.

D.76　If appropriate information is not available to enable the enforcing authority to make such an assessment of relative responsibility (and, following the guidance at paragraph D.36 above, such information cannot reasonably be obtained) the authority should apportion liability in equal shares among the remaining members of the liability group for any significant pollutant linkage, subject to the specific guidance in paragraph D.85 below.

SPECIFIC APPROACHES

Partial Applicability of an Exclusion Test

D.77　If, for any member of the liability group, the circumstances set out in any of the exclusion tests in Part 5 above apply to some extent, but not sufficiently to mean that an exclusion should be made, the enforcing authority should assess that person's degree of responsibility as being reduced to the extent which is appropriate in the light of all the circumstances and the purpose of the test in question. For example, in considering Test 2, a payment may have been made which was sufficient to pay for only half of the necessary remediation at that time — the authority could therefore reduce the payer's responsibility by half.

The Entry of a Substance vs. Its Continued Presence

D.78   In assessing the relative responsibility of a person who has caused or knowingly permitted the entry of a significant pollutant into, onto or under land (the 'first person') and another person who has knowingly permitted the continued presence of that same pollutant in, on or under that land (the 'second person'), the enforcing authority should consider the extent to which the second person had the means and a reasonable opportunity to deal with the presence of the pollutant in question or to reduce the seriousness of the implications of that presence. The authority should then assess the relative responsibilities on the following basis:

(a)   if the second person had the necessary means and opportunity, he should bear the same responsibility as the first person;

(b)   if the second person did not have the means and opportunity, his responsibility relative to that of the first person should be substantially reduced; and

(c)   if the second person had some, but insufficient, means or opportunity, his responsibility relative to that of the first person should be reduced to an appropriate extent.

Persons who have Caused or Knowingly Permitted the Entry of a Significant Pollutant

D.79   Where the enforcing authority is determining the relative responsibilities of members of the liability group who have caused or knowingly permitted the entry of the significant pollutant into, onto or under the land, it should follow the approach set out in paragraphs D.80 to D.83 below.

D.80   If the nature of the remediation action points clearly to different members of the liability group being responsible for particular circumstances at which the action is aimed, the enforcing authority should apportion responsibility in accordance with that indication. In particular, where different persons were in control of different areas of the land in question, and there is no interrelationship between those areas, the enforcing authority should regard the persons in control of the different areas as being separately responsible for the events which make necessary the remediation actions or parts of actions referable to those areas of land.

D.81   If the circumstances in paragraph D.80 above do not apply, but the quantity of the significant pollutant present is a major influence on the cost of remediation, the enforcing authority should regard the relative amounts of that pollutant which are referable to the different persons as an appropriate basis for apportioning responsibility.

D.82   If it is deciding the relative quantities of pollutant which are referable to different persons, the enforcing authority should consider first whether there is direct evidence of the relative quantities referable to each person. If there is such evidence, it should be used. In the absence of direct evidence, the enforcing authority should see whether an appropriate surrogate measure is available. Such surrogate measures can include:

(a)   the relative periods during which the different persons carried out broadly equivalent operations on the land;

(b)   the relative scale of such operations carried out on the land by the different persons (a measure of such scale may be the quantities of a product that were produced);

(c)   the relative areas of land on which different persons carried out their operations; and

(d)   combinations of the foregoing measures.

D.83   In cases where the circumstances in neither paragraph D.80 nor D.81 above apply, the enforcing authority should consider the nature of the activities carried out by the appropriate persons concerned from which the significant pollutant arose. Where these activities were broadly equivalent, the enforcing authority should apportion responsibility in proportion to the periods of time over which the different persons were in control of those activities. It would be appropriate to adjust this apportionment to reflect circumstances where the persons concerned carried out activities which were not broadly equivalent, for example where they were on a different scale.

Persons who have Knowingly Permitted the Continued Presence of a Pollutant

D.84   Where the enforcing authority is determining the relative responsibilities of members of the liability group who have knowingly permitted the continued presence, over a period of time, of a significant pollutant in, on or under land, it should apportion that responsibility in proportion to:

(a)   the length of time during which each person controlled the land;

(b)   the area of land which each person controlled;

(c)   the extent to which each person had the means and a reasonable opportunity to deal with the presence of the pollutant in question or to reduce the seriousness of the implications of that presence; or

(d)   a combination of the foregoing factors.

Companies and Officers

D.85   If, following the application of the exclusion tests (and in particular the specific guidance at paragraphs D.48(k) (iii) and D.49 above) both a company and one or more of its relevant officers remain as members of the liability group, the enforcing authority should apportion liability on the following bases:

(a)   the enforcing authority should treat the company and its relevant officers as a single unit for the purposes of:

(i)   applying the general principle in paragraph D.75 above (ie it should consider the responsibilities of the company and its relevant officers as a whole, in comparison with the responsibilities of other members of the liability group), and

(ii)   making any apportionment required by paragraph D.76 above; and

(b)   having determined the share of liability falling to the company and its relevant officers together, the enforcing authority should apportion responsibility between the company and its relevant officers on a basis which takes into account the degree of personal responsibility of those officers, and the relative levels of resources which may be available to them and to the company to meet the liability.

D.86   For the purposes of paragraph D.85 above, the 'relevant officers' of a company are any director, manager, secretary or other similar officer of the company, or any other person purporting to act in any such capacity.

PART 7   EXCLUSION OF MEMBERS OF A CLASS B LIABILITY GROUP

D.87   The guidance in this Part is issued under section 78F(6) and sets out the test which should be applied in determining whether to exclude from liability a person who would otherwise be a Class B person (that is, a person liable to meet remediation costs solely by reason of ownership or occupation of the land in question). The purpose of the test is to exclude from liability those who do not have an interest in the capital value of the land in question.

D.88   The test applies where two or more persons have been identified as Class B persons for a significant pollutant linkage.

D.89   In such circumstances, the enforcing authority should exclude any Class B person who either:

(a)   occupies the land under a licence, or other agreement, of a kind which has no marketable value or which he is not legally able to assign or transfer to another person (for these purposes the actual marketable value, or the fact that a particular licence or agreement may not actually attract a buyer in the market, are irrelevant); or

(b)   is liable to pay a rent which is equivalent to the rack rent for such of the land in question as he occupies and holds no beneficial interest in that land other than any tenancy to which such rent relates; where the rent is subject to periodic review, the rent should be considered to be equivalent to the rack rent if, at the latest review, it was set at the full market rent at that date.

D.90   However, the test should not be applied, and consequently no exclusion should be made, if it would result in the exclusion of all of the members of the liability group.

PART 8   APPORTIONMENT BETWEEN THE MEMBERS OF A SINGLE CLASS B LIABILITY GROUP

D.91   The statutory guidance in this Part is issued under section 78F(7) and sets out the principles on which liability should be apportioned within each Class B liability group as it stands after any members have been excluded from liability with respect to the relevant significant pollutant linkage as a result of the application of the exclusion test in Part 7.

D.92   Where the whole or part of a remediation action for which a Class B liability group is responsible clearly relates to a particular area within the land to which the significant pollutant linkage as a whole relates, liability for the whole, or the relevant part, of that action should be apportioned amongst those members of the liability group who own or occupy that particular area of land.

D.93   Where those circumstances do not apply, the enforcing authority should apportion liability for the remediation actions necessary for the significant pollutant linkage in question amongst all of the members of the liability group.

D.94   Where the enforcing authority is apportioning liability amongst some or all of the members of a Class B liability group, it should do so in proportion to the capital values of the interests in the land in question, which include those of any buildings or structures on the land:

(a)   where different members of the liability group own or occupy different areas of land, each such member should bear responsibility in the proportion that the capital value of his area of land bears to the aggregate of the capital values of all the areas of land; and

(b)   where different members of the liability group have an interest in the same area of land, each such member should bear responsibility in the proportion which the capital value of his interest bears to the aggregate of the capital values of all those interests; and

(c)   where both the ownership or occupation of different areas of land and the holding of different interests come into the question, the overall liability should first be apportioned between the different areas of land and then between the interests within each of those areas of land, in each case in accordance with the last two sub-paragraphs.

D.95   The capital value used for these purposes should be that estimated by the enforcing authority, on the basis of the available information, disregarding the existence of any contamination. The value should be estimated in relation to the date immediately before the enforcing authority first served a notice under section 78B(3) in relation to that land. Where the land in question is reasonably uniform in nature and amenity and is divided among a number of owner-occupiers, it can be an acceptable approximation of this basis of apportionment to make the apportionment on the basis of the area occupied by each.

D.96   Where part of the land in question is land for which no owner or occupier can be found, the enforcing authority should deduct the share of costs attributable to that land on the basis of the respective capital values of that land and the other land in question before making a determination of liability.

D.97   If appropriate information is not available to enable the enforcing authority to make an assessment of relative capital values (and, following the guidance at paragraph D.36 above, such information cannot reasonably be obtained), the enforcing authority should apportion liability in equal shares among all the members of the liability group.

PART 9 ATTRIBUTION OF RESPONSIBILITY BETWEEN LIABILITY GROUPS

D.98   The statutory guidance in this Part is issued under section 78F(7) and applies where one remediation action is referable to two or more significant pollutant linkages (that is, it is a 'shared action'). This can occur either where both linkages require the same action (that is, it is a 'common action') or where a particular action is part of the best combined remediation scheme for two or more linkages (that is, it is a 'collective action'). This Part provides statutory guidance on the attribution of responsibility for the costs of any shared action between the liability groups for the linkages to which it is referable.

ATTRIBUTING RESPONSIBILITY FOR THE COST OF SHARED ACTIONS BETWEEN LIABILITY GROUPS

D.99   The enforcing authority should attribute responsibility for the costs of any common action among the liability groups for the significant pollutant linkages to which it is referable on the following basis:

(a)   if there is a single Class A liability group, then the full cost of carrying out the common action should be attributed to that group, and no cost should be attributed to any Class B liability group);

(b)   if there are two or more Class A liability groups, then an equal share of the cost of carrying out the common action should be attributed to each of those groups, and no cost should be attributed to any Class B liability group); and

(c)   if there is no Class A liability group and there are two or more Class B liability groups, then the enforcing authority should treat those liability groups as if they formed a single liability group, attributing the cost of carrying out the common action to that combined group, and applying the guidance on exclusion and apportionment set out in Parts 7 and 8 of this Chapter as between all of the members of that combined group.

D.100   The enforcing authority should attribute responsibility for the cost of any collective action among the liability groups for the significant pollutant linkages to which it is referable on the same basis as for the costs of a common action, except that where the costs fall to be divided among several Class A liability groups, instead of being divided equally, they should be attributed on the following basis:

(a)   having estimated the costs of the collective action, the enforcing authority should also estimate the hypothetical cost for each of the liability groups of carrying out the actions which are subsumed by the collective action and which would be necessary if the significant pollutant linkage for which that liability group is responsible were to be addressed separately; these estimates are the 'hypothetical estimates' of each of the liability groups;

(b)   the enforcing authority should then attribute responsibility for the cost of the collective action between the liability groups in the proportions which the hypothetical estimates of each liability group bear to the aggregate of the hypothetical estimates of all the groups.

Confirming the Attribution of Responsibility

D.101   If any appropriate person demonstrates, before the service of a remediation notice, to the satisfaction of the enforcing authority that the result of an attribution made on the basis set out in paragraphs D.99 and D.100 above would have the effect of the liability group of which he is a member having to bear a liability which is so disproportionate (taking into account the overall relative responsibilities of the persons or groups concerned for the condition of the land) as to make the attribution of responsibility between all the liability groups concerned unjust when considered as a whole, the enforcing authority should reconsider the attribution. In doing so, the enforcing authority should consult the other appropriate persons concerned.

D.102   If the enforcing authority then agrees that the original attribution would be unjust it should adjust the attribution between the liability groups so that it is just and fair in the light of all the circumstances. An adjustment under this paragraph should be necessary only in very exceptional cases.

ORPHAN LINKAGES

D.103   As explained above at paragraphs D.12, D.14 and D.17 above, an orphan linkage may arise where:

(a)   the significant pollutant linkage relates solely to the pollution of controlled waters (and not to significant harm) and no Class A person can be found;

(b)   no Class A or Class B persons can be found; or

(c)   those who would otherwise be liable are exempted by one of the relevant statutory provisions (i.e. sections 78J(3), 78K or 78X(3)).

D.104   In any case where only one significant pollutant linkage has been identified, and that is an orphan linkage, the enforcing authority should itself bear the cost of any remediation which is carried out.

D.105   In more complicated cases, there may be two or more significant pollutant linkages, of which some are orphan linkages. Where this applies, the enforcing authority will need to consider each remediation action separately.

D.106   For any remediation action which is referable to an orphan linkage, and is not referable to any other linkage for which there is a liability group, the enforcing authority should itself bear the cost of carrying out that action.

D.107   For any shared action which is referable to an orphan linkage and also to a single significant pollutant linkage for which there is a Class A liability group, the enforcing authority should attribute all of the cost of carrying out that action to that Class A liability group.

D.108   For any shared action which is referable to an orphan linkage and also to two or more significant pollutant linkages for which there are Class A liability groups, the enforcing authority should attribute the costs of carrying out that action between those liability groups in the same way as it would do if the orphan linkage did not exist.

D.109   For any shared action which is referable to an orphan linkage and also to a significant pollutant linkage for which there is a Class B liability group (and not to any significant pollutant linkage for which there is a Class A liability group) the enforcing authority should adopt the following approach:

(a)   where the remediation action is a common action the enforcing authority should attribute all of the cost of carrying out that action to the Class B liability group; and

(b)   where the remediation action is a collective action, the enforcing authority should estimate the hypothetical cost of the action which would be needed to remediate separately the effects of the linkage for which that group is liable. The enforcing authority should then attribute the costs of carrying out the collective action between itself and the Class B liability group so that the expected liability of that group does not exceed that hypothetical cost.

CHAPTER E   STATUTORY GUIDANCE ON THE RECOVERY OF THE COSTS OF REMEDIATION

PART 1   SCOPE OF THE CHAPTER

E.1   The statutory guidance in this Chapter is issued under section 78P(2) of the Environmental Protection Act 1990. It provides guidance on the extent to which the enforcing authority should seek to recover the costs of remediation which it has carried out and which it is entitled to recover.

E.2   Section 78P provides that:

'(1)   Where, by virtue of section 78N(3) (a), (c), (c) or (f) . . . the enforcing authority does any particular thing by way of remediation, it shall be entitled, subject to sections 78J(7) and 78K(6) . . . to recover the reasonable cost incurred in doing it from the appropriate person or, if there are two or more appropriate persons in relation to the thing in question, from those persons in proportions determined pursuant to section 78F(7) . . .

(2)   In deciding whether to recover the cost, and, if so, how much of the cost, which it is entitled to recover under subsection (1) above, the enforcing authority shall have regard—

(a)   to any hardship which the recovery may cause to the person from whom the cost is recoverable; and

(b)   to any guidance issued by the Secretary of State for the purposes of this subsection.'

E.3   The guidance in this Chapter is also crucial in deciding when the enforcing authority is prevented from serving a remediation notice. Under section 78H(5), the enforcing authority may not serve a remediation notice if the authority has the power to carry out remediation itself, by virtue of section 78N. Under that latter section, the authority asks the hypothetical question of whether it would seek to recover all of the reasonable costs it would incur if it carried out the remediation itself. The authority then has the power to carry out that remediation itself if it concludes that, having regard to hardship and the guidance in this chapter, it would either not seek to recover its costs, or seek to recover only a part of its costs.

E.4   Section 78H(5) provides that:

'(5)   The enforcing authority shall not serve a remediation notice on a person if and so long as ...

(d)   the authority is satisfied that the powers conferred on it by section 78N below to do what is appropriate by way of remediation are exercisable ...'

E.5   Section 78N(3) provides that the enforcing authority has the power to carry out remediation:

'(e)   where the enforcing authority considers that were it to do some particular thing by way of remediation, it would decide, by virtue of subsection (2) of section 78P ... or any guidance issued under that subsection,

(i)   not to seek to recover under subsection (1) of that section any of the reasonable cost incurred by it in doing that thing., or

(ii)   to seek so to recover only a portion of that cost; ...'

E.6   The enforcing authority is required to have regard to the statutory guidance in this Chapter.

PART 2   DEFINITION OF TERMS

E.7   Unless otherwise stated, any word, term or phrase given a specific meaning in Part IIA of the Environmental Protection Act 1990, or in the statutory guidance in Chapters A, B, C, or D has the same meaning for the purpose of the guidance in this Chapter.

E.8   In addition, for the purposes of the statutory guidance in this Chapter, the term 'cost recovery decision' is used to describe any decision by the enforcing authority, for the purposes either of section 78P or of sections 78H and 78N, whether:

(a)   to recover from the appropriate person all of the reasonable costs incurred by the authority in carrying out remediation; or

(b)   not to recover those costs or to recover only part of those costs (described below as 'waiving or reducing its cost recovery').

E.9   Any reference to 'Part IIA' means 'Part IIA of the Environmental Protection Act 1990'. Any reference to a 'section' in primary legislation means a section of the Environmental Protection Act 1990, unless it is specifically stated otherwise.

PART 3   COST RECOVERY DECISIONS

COST RECOVERY DECISIONS IN GENERAL

E.10   The statutory guidance in this Part sets out considerations to which the enforcing authority should have regard when making any cost recovery decision. In view of the wide variation in situations which are likely to arise, including the history and ownership of land, and liability for its remediation, the statutory guidance in this Chapter sets out principles and approaches, rather than detailed rules. The enforcing authority will need to have regard to the circumstances of each individual case.

E.11   In making any cost recovery decision, the enforcing authority should have regard to the following general principles:

(a)   the authority should aim for an overall result which is as fair and equitable as possible to all who may have to meet the costs of remediation, including national and local taxpayers; and

(b)   the 'polluter pays' principle, by virtue of which the costs of remediating pollution are to be borne by the polluter; the authority should therefore consider the degree and nature of responsibility of the appropriate person for the creation, or continued existence, of the circumstances which lead to the land in question being identified as contaminated land.

E.12   In general, this will mean that the enforcing authority should seek to recover in full its reasonable costs. However, the authority should waive or reduce the recovery of costs to the extent that the authority considers this appropriate and reasonable, either:

(a)   to avoid any hardship which the recovery may cause to the appropriate person; or

(b)   to reflect one or more of the specific considerations set out in the statutory guidance in Parts 4, 5 and 6 below.

E.13   When deciding how much of its costs it should recover in any case, the enforcing authority should consider whether it could recover more of its costs by deferring recovery and securing them by a charge on the land in question under section 78P. Such deferral may lead to payment from the appropriate person either in instalments (see section 78P(12)) or when the land is next sold.

INFORMATION FOR MAKING DECISIONS

E.14   In general, the enforcing authority should expect anyone who is seeking a waiver or reduction in the recovery of remediation costs to present any information needed to support his request.

E.15   In making any cost recovery decision, the authority should always consider any relevant information provided by the appropriate person. The authority should also seek to obtain such information as is reasonable, having regard to:

(a)   how the information might be obtained;

(b)   the cost, for all the parties involved, of obtaining the information; and

(c)   the potential significance of the information for any decision.

E.16   The enforcing authority should, in all cases, inform the appropriate person of any cost recovery decisions taken, explaining the reasons for those decisions.

COST RECOVERY POLICIES

E.17   In order to promote transparency, fairness and consistency, an enforcing authority which is a local authority may wish to prepare, adopt and make available as appropriate a policy statement about the general approach it intends to follow in making cost recovery decisions. This would outline circumstances in which it would waive or reduce cost recovery (and thereby, by inference, not serve a remediation notice because it has the powers to carry out the remediation itself), having had regard to hardship and the statutory guidance in this Chapter.

E.18   Were the Environment Agency is making a cost recovery decision with respect to a special site falling within the area of a local authority which has adopted such a policy statement, the Agency should take account of that statement.

PART 4   CONSIDERATIONS APPLYING BOTH TO CLASS A AND CLASS B PERSONS

E.19   The statutory guidance in this Part sets out considerations to which the enforcing authority should have regard when making any cost recovery decisions, irrespective of whether the appropriate person is a Class A person of a Class B person (as defined in Chapter D). They apply in addition to the general issue of the 'hardship' which the cost recovery may cause to the appropriate person.

COMMERCIAL ENTERPRISES

E.20   Subject to the specific guidance elsewhere in this Chapter, the enforcing authority should adopt the same approach to all types of commercial or industrial enterprises which are identified as appropriate persons. This applies whether the appropriate person is a public corporation, a limited company (whether public or private), a partnership (whether limited or not) or an individual operating as a sole trader.

Threat of Business Closure or Insolvency

E.21   In the case of a small or medium-sized enterprise which is the appropriate person, or which is run by the appropriate person, the enforcing authority should consider:

(a)   whether recovery of the full cost attributable to that person would mean that the enterprise is likely to become insolvent and thus cease to exist; and

(b)   if so, the cost to the local economy of such a closure.

E.22   Where the cost of closure appears to be greater than the costs of remediation which the enforcing authority would have to bear themselves, the authority should consider waiving or reducing its costs recovery to the extent needed to avoid making the enterprise insolvent.

E.23   However, the authority should not waive or reduce its costs recovery where:

(a)   it is clear that an enterprise has deliberately arranged matters so as to avoid responsibility for the costs of remediation;

(b)   it appears that the enterprise would be likely to become insolvent whether or not recovery of the full cost takes place; or

(c)   it appears that the enterprise could be kept in, or returned to, business even if it does become insolvent under its current ownership.

E.24   For these purposes, a 'small or medium-sized enterprise' is as defined in the European Commission's Community Guidelines on State Aid for Small and Medium-Sized Enterprises, published in the Official Journal of the European

Communities (the reference number for the present version of the guidelines is OJ C213 1996 item 4). This can be summarised as an independent enterprise with fewer than 250 employees, and either an annual turnover not exceeding €40 million, or an annual balance sheet total not exceeding €27 million.

E.25   Where the enforcing authority is a local authority, it may wish to take account in any such cost recovery decisions of any policies it may have for assisting enterprise or promoting economic development (for example, for granting financial or other assistance under section 33 of the Local Government and Housing Act 1989, including any strategy which it has published under section 35 of that Act concerning the use of such powers).

E.26   Here the Environment Agency is the enforcing authority, it should seek to be consistent with the local authority in whose area the contaminated land in question is situated. The Environment Agency should therefore consult the local authority, and should take that authority's views into consideration in making its own cost recovery decision.

TRUSTS

E.27   Where the appropriate persons include persons acting as trustees, the enforcing authority should assume that such trustees will exercise all the powers which they have, or may reasonably obtain, to make funds available from the trust, or from borrowing that can be made on behalf of the trust, for the purpose of paying for remediation. The authority should, nevertheless, consider waiving or reducing its costs recovery to the extent that the costs of remediation to be recovered from the trustees would otherwise exceed the amount that can be made available from the trust to cover those costs.

E.28   However, as exceptions to the approach set out in the preceding paragraph, the authority should not waive or reduce its costs recovery:

(a)   where it is clear that the trust was formed for the purpose of avoiding paying the costs of remediation; or

(b)   to the extent that trustees have personally benefited, or will personally benefit, from the trust.

CHARITIES

E.29   Since charities are intended to operate for the benefit of the community, the enforcing authority should consider the extent to which any recovery of costs from a charity would jeopardise that charity's ability to continue to provide a benefit or amenity which is in the public interest. Where this is the case, the authority should consider waiving or reducing its costs recovery to the extent needed to avoid such a consequence. This approach applies equally to charitable trusts and to charitable companies.

SOCIAL HOUSING LANDLORDS

E.30   The enforcing authority should consider waiving or reducing its costs recovery if.

(a)   the appropriate person is a body eligible for registration as a social housing landlord under section 2 of the Housing Act 1996 (for example, a housing association);

(b)   its liability relates to land used for social housing; and

(c)   full recovery would lead to financial difficulties for the appropriate person, such that the provision or upkeep of the social housing would be jeopardised.

E.31   The extent of the waiver or reduction should be sufficient to avoid any such financial difficulties.

PART 5   SPECIFIC CONSIDERATIONS APPLYING TO CLASS A PERSONS

E.32   The statutory guidance in this Part sets out specific considerations to which the enforcing authority should have regard in cost recovery decisions where the appropriate person is a Class A person, as defined in Chapter D (that is, a person who has caused or knowingly permitted the significant pollutant to be in, on or under the contaminated land).

E.33   In applying the approach in this Part, the enforcing authority should be less willing to waive or reduce its costs recovery where it was in the course of carrying on a business that the Class A person caused or knowingly permitted the presence of the significant pollutants, than where he was not carrying on a business. This is because in the former case he is likely to have earned profits from the activity which created or permitted the presence of those pollutants.

WHERE OTHER POTENTIALLY APPROPRIATE PERSONS HAVE NOT BEEN FOUND

E.34   In some cases where a Class A person has been found, it may be possible to identify another person who caused or knowingly permitted the presence of the significant pollutant in question, but who cannot now be found for the purposes of treating him as an appropriate person. For example, this might apply where a company has been dissolved.

E.35   The authority should consider waiving or reducing its costs recovery from a Class A person if that person demonstrates to the satisfaction of the enforcing authority that:

(a)   another identified person, who cannot now be found, also caused or knowingly permitted the significant pollutant to be in, on or under the land; and

(b)   if that other person could be found, the Class A person seeking the waiver or reduction of the authority's costs recovery would either:

(i)   be excluded from liability by virtue of one or more of the exclusion tests set out in Part 5 of Chapter D, or

(ii)   the proportion of the cost of remediation which the appropriate person has to bear would have been significantly less, by virtue of the guidance on apportionment set out in Part 6 of Chapter D.

E.36   Where an appropriate person is making a case for the authority's costs recovery to be waived or reduced by virtue of paragraph E.35 above, the enforcing authority should expect that person to provide evidence that a particular person, who cannot now be found, caused or knowingly permitted the significant pollutant to be in, on or under the land. The enforcing authority should not regard it as sufficient for the appropriate person concerned merely to state that such a person must have existed.

PART 6 SPECIFIC CONSIDERATIONS APPLYING TO CLASS B PERSONS

E.37 The statutory guidance in this Part sets out specific considerations relating to cost recovery decisions where the appropriate person is a Class B person, as defined in Chapter D (that is, a person who is liable by virtue or their ownership or occupation of the contaminated land, but who has not caused or knowingly permitted the significant pollutant to be in, on or under the land).

COSTS IN RELATION TO LAND VALUES

E.38 In some cases, the costs of remediation may exceed the value of the land in its current use (as defined in Chapter A) after the required remediation has been carried out.

E.39 The enforcing authority should consider waiving or reducing its costs recovery from a Class B person if that person demonstrates to the satisfaction of the authority that the costs of remediation are likely to exceed the value of the land. In this context, the 'value' should be taken to be the value that the remediated land would have on the open market, at the time the cost recovery decision is made, disregarding any possible blight arising from the contamination.

E.40 In general, the extent of the waiver or reduction in costs recovery should be sufficient to ensure that the costs of remediation borne by the Class B person do not exceed the value of the land. However, the enforcing authority should seek to recover more of its costs to the extent that the remediation would result in an increase in the value of any other land from which the Class B person would benefit.

PRECAUTIONS TAKEN BEFORE ACQUIRING A FREEHOLD OR A LEASEHOLD INTEREST

E.41 In some cases, the appropriate person may have been reckless as to the possibility that land he has acquired may be contaminated, or he may have decided to take a risk that the land was not contaminated. On the other hand, he may have taken precautions to ensure that he did not acquire land which is contaminated.

E.42 The authority should consider reducing its costs recovery where a Class B person who is the owner of the land demonstrates to the satisfaction of the authority that:

(a) he took such steps prior to acquiring the freehold, or accepting the grant of assignment of a leasehold, as would have been reasonable at that time to establish the presence of any pollutants;

(b) when he acquired the land, or accepted the grant of assignment of the leasehold, he was nonetheless unaware of the presence of the significant pollutant now identified and could not reasonably have been expected to have been aware of their presence; and

(c)   it would be fair and reasonable, taking into account the interests of national and local taxpayers, that he should not bear the whole cost of remediation.

E.43   The enforcing authority should bear in mind that the safeguards which might reasonably be expected to be taken will be different in different types of transaction (for example, acquisition of recreational land as compared with commercial land transactions) and as between buyers of different types (for example, private individuals as compared with major commercial undertakings).

OWNER-OCCUPIERS OF DWELLINGS

E.44   Where a Class B person owns and occupies a dwelling on the contaminated land in question, the enforcing authority should consider waiving or reducing its costs recovery where that person satisfies the authority that, at the time the person purchased the dwelling, he did not know, and could not reasonably have been expected to have known, that the land was adversely affected by presence of a pollutant.

E.45   Any such waiver or reduction should be to the extent needed to ensure that the Class B person in question bears no more of the cost of remediation than it appears reasonable to impose, having regard to his income, capital and outgoings. Where the appropriate person has inherited the dwelling or received it as a gift, the approach in paragraph E.44 above should be applied with respect to the time at which he received the property.

E.46   Where the contaminated land in question extends beyond the dwelling and its curtilage, and is owned or occupied by the same appropriate person, the approach in paragraph E.44 above should be applied only to the dwelling and its curtilage.

The Housing Renewal Grant Analogy

E.47   In judging the extent of a waiver or reduction in costs recovery from an owner-occupier of a dwelling, an enforcing authority which is a local authority may wish to apply an approach analogous to that used for applications for housing renovation grant (HRG). These grants are assessed on a means-tested basis, as presently set out in the Housing Renewal Grants Regulations 1996 (S.I. 1996/2890, as amended). The HRG test determines how much a person should contribute towards the cost of necessary renovation work for which they are responsible, taking into account income, capital and outgoings, including allowances for those with particular special needs.

E.48   The HRG approach can be applied as if the appropriate person were applying for HRG and the authority had decided that the case was appropriate for grant assessment. Using this analogy, the authority would conclude that costs recovery should be waived or reduced to the extent that the appropriate person contributes no more thin if the work were house renovations for which HRG was being sought. For this purpose, any upper limits for grants payable under HRG should be ignored.

E.49   Where the Environment Agency is the enforcing authority, it should seek to be consistent with the local authority in whose area the contaminated land in question is situated. Tne Environment Agency should therefore consult the local authority, and should take that authority's views into consideration in making its own cost recovery decision.

ANNEX 5

GUIDE TO THE ENVIRONMENT ACT 1995 (COMMENCEMENT NO. 16 AND SAVING PROVISION) (ENGLAND) ORDER 2000

Commencement of Part IIA Environmental Protection Act 1990

1.   The Environment Act 1995 (Commencement No. 1) Order 1995 (S.I. 1995/ 1983) brought into force section 57 of the Environment Act 1995 ('the 1995 Act'), in so far as was necessary to enable the Secretary of State to consult on and issue statutory guidance and make regulations.

2.   The main effect of the Environment Act 1995 (Commencement No.16 and Saving Provision) (England) Order 2000 (S.I. 2000/340(C.8)) is to bring the remainder of section 57 of the 1995 Act into force in England on 1 April 2000. This, in turn, brings the Part IIA regime into force.

Repeals and Other Amendments to the 1990 Act

3.   The Order also brings into force the following amendments to the 1990 Act:

(a)   amendments to the definition of a statutory nuisance in section 79, so as to exclude any matter which consists of, or is caused by, land in a contaminated state;

(b)   the repeal of the following sections (neither of which ever came into force):

(i)   section 61, which would have created specific duties for waste regulation authorities as respects closed landfills, and

(ii)   section 143, which would have required local authorities to compile registers of land which may be contaminated; and

(c)   an amendment to section 161, relating to the use of the affirmative resolution procedure for any order under the new section 78M(4), (which deals with changes to the maximum level of fines for non-compliance with remediation notices).

Saving Provision Relating to Statutory Nuisance

4.   Article 3 of the Order makes a saving provision with respect to the dis-application of the statutory nuisance regime from land contamination problems. This has the effect of ensuring that any regulatory action which had commenced before 1 April 2000 can continue.

ANNEX 6

GLOSSARY OF TERMS

The statutory guidance (and other parts of this Circular) uses a number of terms which are defined in Part IIA of the 1990 Act, other Acts or in the guidance itself. The meanings of the most important of these terms are set out below, along with a reference to the section in the Act or the paragraph in which the relevant term is defined.

Terms which are defined in statutes (mostly in section 78A of the 1990 Act) are shown with underlining.

Animal or crop effect: significant harm of a type listed in box 3 of Table A of Chapter A.

Apportionment: any determination by the enforcing authority under section 78F(7) (that is, a division of the costs of carrying out any remediation action between two or more appropriate persons). *Paragraph D.5(e)*

Appropriate person: defined in section 78A(9) as:
'any person who is an appropriate person, determined in accordance with section 78E ..., to bear responsibility for any thing which is to be done by way of remediation in any particular case.'

Assessment action: a remediation action falling within the definition of remediation in section 78A(7)(a), that is the doing of anything for the purpose of assessing the condition of the contaminated land in question, or any controlled waters affected by that land or any land adjoining or adjacent to that land. *Paragraph C.8(e)*

Attribution: the process of apportionment between liability groups. *Paragraph D.5(e)*

Building: any structure or erection, and any part of a building including any part below ground, but not including plant or machinery comprised in a building. *Table A*

Building effect: significant harm of a type listed in box 4 of Table A of Chapter A.

Caused or knowingly permitted: test for establishing responsibility for remediation, under section 78F(2); see paragraphs 9.8 to 9.14 of Annex 2 for a discussion of the interpretation of this term.

Changes to Substances: an exclusion test for Class A persons set out in Part 5 of Chapter D. *Paragraphs D.62 to D.64*

Charging notice: a notice placing a legal charge on land served under section 78P(3)(b) by an enforcing authority to enable the authority to recover from the appropriate person any reasonable cost incurred by the authority in carrying out remediation.

Class A liability group: a liability group consisting of one or more Class A persons. *Paragraph D.5 (c)*

Class A person: a person who is an appropriate person by virtue of section 78F(2) (that is, because he has caused or knowingly permitted a pollutant to be in, on or under the land). *Paragraph D.5 (a)*

Class B liability group: a liability group consisting of one or more Class B persons. *Paragraph D.5(c)*

Class B person: a person who is an appropriate person by virtue of section 78F(4) or (5) (that is, because he is the owner or occupier of the land in circumstances where no Class A person can be found with respect to a particular remediation action). *Paragraph D.5(b)*

Collective action: a remediation action which addresses together all of the significant pollution linkages to which it is referable, but which would not have been part of the remediation package for every one of those linkages if each of them had been addressed separately. *Paragraph D.22(b)*

Common action: a remediation action which addresses together all of the significant pollution linkages to which it is referable, and which would have been part of the remediation package for each of those linkages if each of them had been addressed separately. *Paragraph D.22 (a)*

Contaminant: a substance which is in, on or under the land and which has the potential to cause harm or to cause pollution of controlled waters. *Paragraph A.12*

<u>**Contaminated land**</u>: defined in section 78A(2) as

'any land which appears to the local authority in whose area it is situated to be in such a condition, by reason of substances in, on or under the land, that—

(a)   significant harm is being caused or there is a significant possibility of such harm being caused, or;

(b)   pollution of controlled waters is being, or is likely to be, caused.'

Contaminated Land (England) Regulations 2000: regulations (S.I. 2000/227) made under Part IIA — described in Annex 4.

<u>**Controlled waters**</u>: defined in section 78A(9) by reference to Part III (section 104) of   the Water Resources Act 1991; this embraces territorial and coastal waters, inland   fresh waters, and ground waters.

Cost recovery decision: any decision by the enforcing authority whether:

(a)   to recover from the appropriate person all the reasonable costs incurred by the authority in carrying out remediation, or

(b)   not to recover those costs or to recover only part of those costs. *Paragraph E.8*

Current use: any use which is currently being made, or is likely to be made, of the land and which is consistent with any existing planning permission (or is otherwise lawful under town and country planning legislation). This definition is subject to the following qualifications:

(a)   the current use should be taken to include any temporary use, permitted under town and country planning legislation, to which the land is, or is likely to be, put from time to time;

(b)   the current use includes future uses or developments which do not require a new, or amended, grant of planning permission;

(c)   the current use should, nevertheless, be taken to include any likely informal recreational use of the land, whether authorised by the owners or occupiers or not, (for example, children playing on the land); however, in assessing the likelihood of any such informal use, the local authority should give due attention to measures taken to prevent or restrict access to the land, and

(d)   in the case of agricultural land, however, the current agricultural use should not be taken to extend beyond the growing or rearing of the crops or animals which are habitually grown or reared on the land. *Paragraph A.26*

Ecological system effect: significant harm of a type listed in box 2 of Table A of Chapter A.

Enforcing authority defined in section 78A(9) as:

(a)   in relation to a special site, the Environment Agency;

(b)   in relation to contaminated land other than a special site, the local authority in whose area the land is situated.

Escaped Substances: an exclusion test for Class A persons set out in Part 5 of Chapter D. *Paragraphs D.65 to D.67*

Excluded Activities: an exclusion test for Class A persons set out in Part 5 of Chapter D. *Paragraphs D.47 to D.50*

Exclusion: any determination by the enforcing authority under section 78F(6) (that is, that a person is to be treated as not being an appropriate person). *Paragraph D.5(d)*

Favourable conservation status: defined in Article 1 of Council Directive 92/43/EEC on the conservation of natural habitats and of wild fauna and flora.

Hardship: a factor underlying any cost recovery decision made by an enforcing authority under section 78P(2). See paragraphs 10.8 to 10.10 of Annex 2 for a discussion of the interpretation of this term.

Harm: defined in section 78A(4) as:

'harm to the health of living organisms or other interference with the ecological systems of which they form part and, in the case of man, includes harm to his property.'

Human health effect: significant harm of a type listed in box 1 of Table A of Chapter A.

Industrial, trade or business premises: defined in section 78M(6), for the purpose of determining the penalty for failure to comply with a remediation notice, as:

'premises used for any industrial, trade or business purposes or premises not so used on which matter is burnt in connection with any industrial, trade or business process, and premises are used for industrial purposes where they are used for the purposes of any treatment or process as well as where they are used for the purpose of manufacturing.'

Inspection using statutory powers of entry: any detailed inspection of land carried out through use of powers of entry given to an enforcing authority by section 108 of the Environment Act 1995. *Paragraph B. 21*

Introduction of Pathways or Receptors: an exclusion test for Class A persons set out in Part 5 of Chapter D. *Paragraphs D.68 to D.72*

Intrusive investigation: an investigation of land (for example by exploratory excavations) which involves actions going beyond simple visual inspection of the land, limited sampling or assessment of documentary information. *Paragraph B.20(c)*

Liability group: the persons who are appropriate persons with respect to a particular significant pollutant linkage. *Paragraph D.5(c)*

Local authority: defined in section 78A(9) as meaning any unitary authority, district council, the Common Council of the City of London, the Sub-Treasurer of the Inner Temple and the Under-Treasurer of the Middle Temple.

Monitoring action: a remediation action falling within the definition in section 78A(7) (c), that is 'making of subsequent inspections from time to time for the purpose of keeping under review the condition of the land or waters'. *Paragraph C.8(g)*

Orphan linkage: a significant pollutant linkage for which no appropriate person can be found, or where those who would otherwise be liable are exempted by one of the relevant statutory provisions. *Paragraphs D.12, D.14 and D.1 7*

Owner: defined in section 78A(9) as:
'a person (other than a mortgagee not in possession) who, whether in his own right or as trustee for any other person, is entitled to receive the rack rent of the land, or where the land is not let at a rack rent, would be so entitled if it were so let.'

Part IIA: Part IIA of the Environmental Protection Act 1990.

Pathway: one or more routes or means by, or through, which a receptor:
    (a)   is being exposed to, or affected by, a contaminant, or
    (b)   could be so exposed or affected. *Paragraph A.14*

Payments Made for Remediation: an exclusion test for Class A persons set out in Part 5 of Chapter D. *Paragraphs D.51 to D.56*

Person acting in a relevant capacity: defined in section 78X(4), for the purposes of limiting personal liability, as any of the following:
    '(a)   a person acting as an insolvency practitioner, within the meaning of section 388 of the Insolvency Act 1986 (including that section as it applies in relation to an insolvent partnership by virtue of any order made under section 421 of that Act;
    (b)   the official receiver acting in a capacity in which he would be regarded as acting as an insolvency practitioner within the meaning of section 388 of the Insolvency Act 1986 if subsection (5) of that section were disregarded;
    (c)   the official receiver acting as a receiver or manager;
    (d)   a person acting as a special manager under section 177 or 370 of the Insolvency Act 1986; ...
    (f)   a person acting as a receiver or receiver and manager under or by virtue of any enactment, or by virtue of his appointment as such by an order of a court or by any other instrument.'

Pollutant: a contaminant which forms part of a pollutant linkage. *Paragraph A.17*

Pollutant linkage: the relationship between a contaminant, a pathway and a receptor. *Paragraph A.17*

Pollution of controlled waters: defined in section 78A(9) as:
'the entry into controlled waters of any poisonous, noxious or polluting matter or any solid waste matter.'

Possibility of significant harm: a measure of the probability, or frequency, of the occurrence of circumstances which would lead to significant harm being caused. *Paragraph A. 27*

Receptor: either:

(a)   a living organism, a group of living organisms, an ecological system or a piece of property which:

(i)   is in a category listed in Table A in Chapter A as a type of receptor, and

(ii)   is being, or could be, harmed, by a contaminant; or

(b)   controlled waters which are being, or could be, polluted by a contaminant. *Paragraph A. 13*

Register: the public register maintained by the enforcing authority under section 78R of particulars relating to contaminated land.

Related companies: are those which are, or were at the 'relevant date', members of a group of companies consisting of a 'holding company' and its 'subsidiaries'. The 'relevant date' is that on which the enforcing authority first served on anyone a notice under section 78B(3) identifying the land as contaminated land, and the terms 'holding company' and 'subsidiaries' have the same meaning as in section 736 of the Companies Act 1985. *Paragraph D.46*

Relevant information: information relating to the assessment of whether there is a significant possibility of significant harm being caused, which is:

(a)   scientifically-based;

(b)   authoritative;

(c)   relevant to the assessment of risks arising from the presence of contaminants in soil; and

(d)   appropriate to the determination of whether any land is contaminated land for the purposes of Part IIA, in that the use of the information is consistent with providing a level of protection of risk in line with the qualitative criteria set out in Tables A and B of Chapter A. *Paragraph A. 31*

Relevant land or waters: the contaminated land in question, any controlled waters affected by that land and any land adjoining or adjacent to the contaminated land on which remediation might be required as a consequence of the contaminated land being such land. *Paragraph C.8(d)*

Remedial treatment action: a remediation action falling within the definition in section 78A(7)(b), that is the doing of any works, the carrying out of any operations or the taking of any steps in relation to any such land or waters for the purpose:

(a)   of preventing or minimising, or remedying or mitigating the effects of any significant harm, or any pollution of controlled waters, by reason of which the contaminated land is such land, or

(b)   of restoring the land or waters to their former state. *Paragraph C.8(f)*

Remediation: defined in section 78A(7) as

'(a)   the doing of anything for the purpose of assessing the condition of—

(i)   the contaminated land in question;

(ii)   any controlled waters affected by that land; or

(iii)   any land adjoining or adjacent to that land;

(b)   the doing of any works, the carrying out of any operations or the taking of any steps in relation to any such land or waters for the purpose—

(i)   of preventing or minimising, or remedying or mitigating the effects of any significant harm, or any pollution of controlled waters, by reason of which the contaminated land is such land; or

(ii)   of restoring the land or waters to their former state; or

(c)   the making of subsequent inspections from time to time for the purpose of keeping under review the condition of the land or waters.'

Remediation action: any individual thing which is being, or is to be, done by way of remediation. *Paragraph C.8(a)*

Remediation declaration: defined in section 78H(6). It is a document prepared and published by the enforcing authority recording remediation actions which it would have specified in a remediation notice, but which it is precluded from specifying by virtue of sections 78E(4) or (5), the reasons why it would have specified those actions and the grounds on which it is satisfied that it is precluded from specifying them in a notice.

Remediation notice: defined in section 78E(1) as a notice specifying what an appropriate person is to do by way of remediation and the periods within which he is required to do each of the things so specified.

Remediation package: the full set or sequence of remediation actions, within a remediation scheme, which are referable to a particular significant pollutant linkage. *Paragraph C.8(b)*

Remediation scheme: the complete set or sequence of remediation actions (referable to one or more significant pollutant linkages) to be carried out with respect to the relevant land or waters. *Paragraph C.8(c)*

Remediation statement: defined in section 78H(7). It is a statement prepared and published by the responsible person detailing the remediation actions which are being, have been, or are expected to be, done as well as the periods within which these things are being done.

Risk: the combination of:

(a)   the probability, or frequency, of occurrence of a defined hazard (for example, exposure to a property of a substance with the potential to cause harm); and

(b)   the magnitude (including the seriousness) of the consequences. *Paragraph A.9*

Shared action: a remediation action which is referable to the significant pollutant in more than one significant pollutant linkage. *Paragraph D.21(b)*

Single-linkage action: a remediation action which is referable solely to the significant pollutant in a single significant pollutant linkage. *Paragraph D.21(a)*

Significant harm: defined in section 78A(5). It means any harm which is determined to be significant in accordance with the statutory guidance in Chapter A (that is, it meets one of the descriptions of types of harm in the second column of Table A of that Chapter).

Significant pollutant: a pollutant which forms part of a significant pollutant linkage. *Paragraph A.20*

Significant pollutant linkage: a pollutant linkage which forms the basis for a determination that a piece of land is contaminated land. *Paragraph A.20*

Significant possibility of significant harm: a possibility of significant harm being caused which, by virtue of section 78A(5), is determined to be significant in accordance with the statutory guidance in Chapter A.

Sold with Information: an exclusion test for Class A persons set out in Part 5 of Chapter D. *Paragraph D.57 to D.61*

Special site: defined by section 78A(3) as:

'any contaminated land—

(a)   which has been designated as such a site by virtue of section 78C(7) or 78D(6) . . .; and

(b)   whose designation as such has not been terminated by the appropriate Agency under section 78Q(4) . . .'.

The effect of the designation of any contaminated land as a special site is that the Environment Agency, rather than the local authority, becomes the enforcing authority for the land.

Substance: defined in section 78A(9) as:

'any natural or artificial substance, whether in solid or liquid form or in the form of a gas or vapour.'

Index